DISCOVER more about how you can
LAUGH & COLOR
your way to better health and greater happiness at
www.SeriousGiggles.com

SHARE your colored masterpieces or
SUBMIT your new creations
for possible inclusion in my next book
www.LaughterDoodles.com

Follow me on Twitter @LaughterDoodles
"Like" **https://www.facebook.com/LaughterDoodles**

Cover Design by Monica Routman

Special Thanks to
Monica Routman, Rachael Siegelman & Shelli Diamond
& the many friends who offered
oodles of color-felt feedback,
fun and laughter along the way!

Laugh for your health

FACT: Letting your lips curl into a smile sends endorphins to your brain, changing your body chemistry, making you happier. You don't need to think something's funny. Just the sheer act of smiling will do it!

Your body doesn't know the difference between intentional or spontaneous laughter. Laughter releases chemicals in your body that help reduce stress, anxiety and depression.

In my laughter sessions, we use creativity and laughter to become more childlike and silly, getting more focused and grounded in the process.

Color for your health

FACT: Founder of analytical psychology, Carl Jung, prescribed coloring to patients suffering from anxiety as a way to get calmer and more centered.

Today, adult coloring clubs are sprouting up all over as stress and anxiety seem to be taking over our lives.

Laugh and Color for better health

The benefits of coloring include: relaxation, de-stressing, accomplishment and taking a break. Smile and laugh while you color, and you'll become happier while improving your health. So, go ahead...

- Grab your coloring tools
- Find a place of calm
- Let out your inner child
- Encourage your creativity to flow
- Laugh yourself into a great mood…and have OODLES of FUN!

Please share your Laughter Doodles coloring experience with me on my website: www.LaughterDoodles.com
For more information about how you can add more healthy laughter to your life, visit: www.SeriousGiggles.com

LAUGHTER DOODLES are OODLES of FUN!

Set your imagination free with a coloring book that inspires transformation. Everyone knows that laughter is the best medicine, so sit back and smile as this quirky set of doodles evokes a happier and healthier you.

Please send me your favorite colored creations for an opportunity to be featured on LaughterDoodles.com where I'll regularly showcase amazing examples of YOUR happy imagination. (Sarah@SeriousGiggles.com)

Join our LaughterDoodles community on Facebook where you can:

- Learn how laughter can help you build resilience and turn stress and challenges into opportunities.

- Chat with others who are building laughter into their lives for better health.

- Post questions to "Ask Sarah" and get personalized coaching tips on how laughter can improve specific situations in your life.

- Enjoy the support of an inspiring, caring community led by nationally recognized laughter specialist, Sarah Routman. (www.facebook.com/LaughterDoodles)

If you feel inspired to create your own LAUGHTER DOODLE for possible inclusion in my next LAUGHTER DOODLE coloring book, send to me. (Sarah@SeriousGiggles.com)

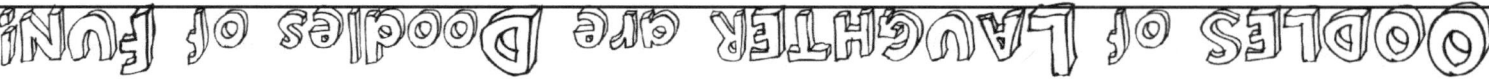

OODLES of LAUGHTER are Doodles of FUN!

Look for: *Laughter Doodles & Oodles of Fun - Your Very Own Laughter Companion.*

A cross between a journal and a workbook, this beautiful volume is designed to help you infuse more intentional Laughter, resilience and better health in your life. (www.SeriousGiggles.com)

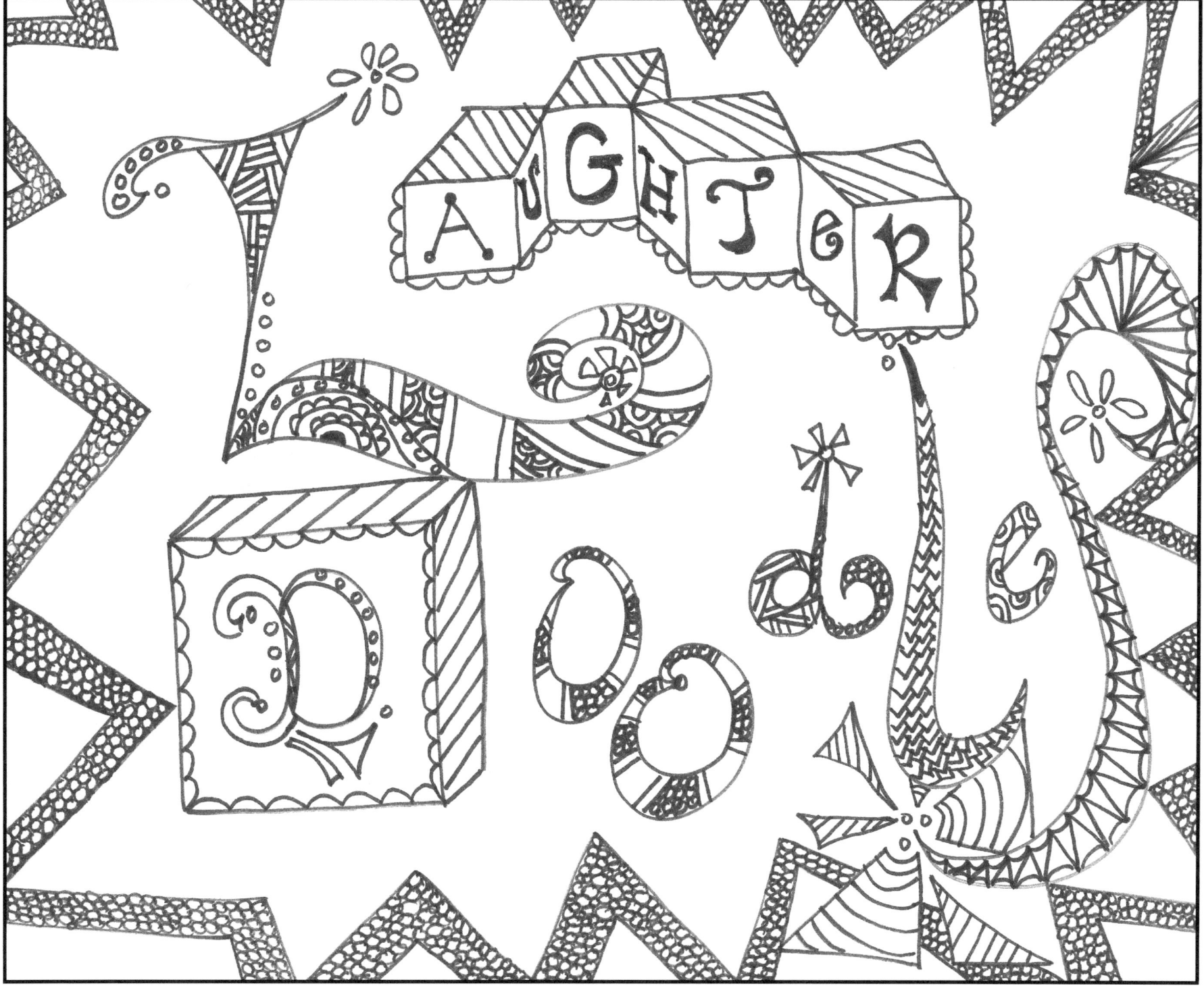

LAUGH while you color ... and breathe deeply

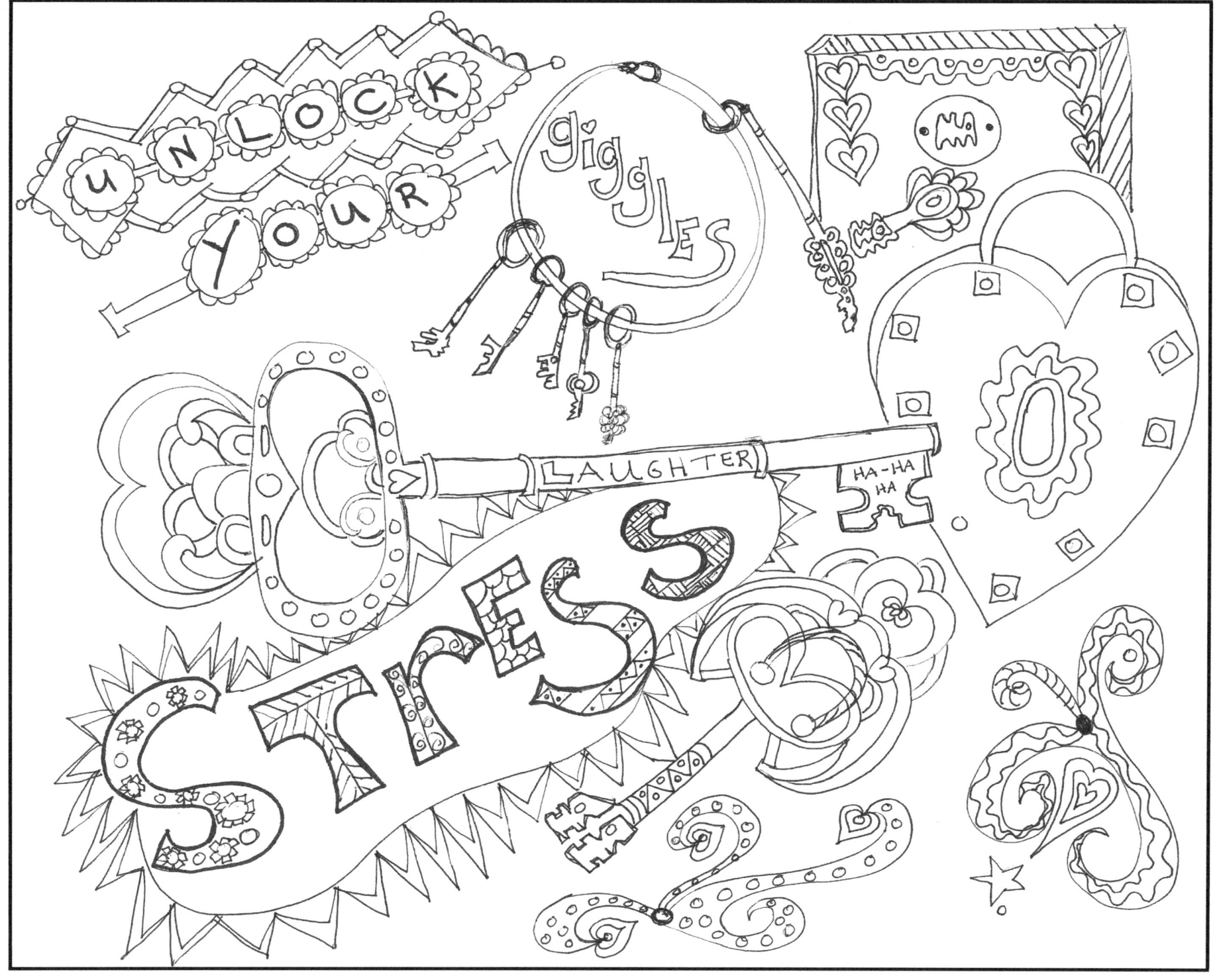

LAUGH while you color ... and improve your mood

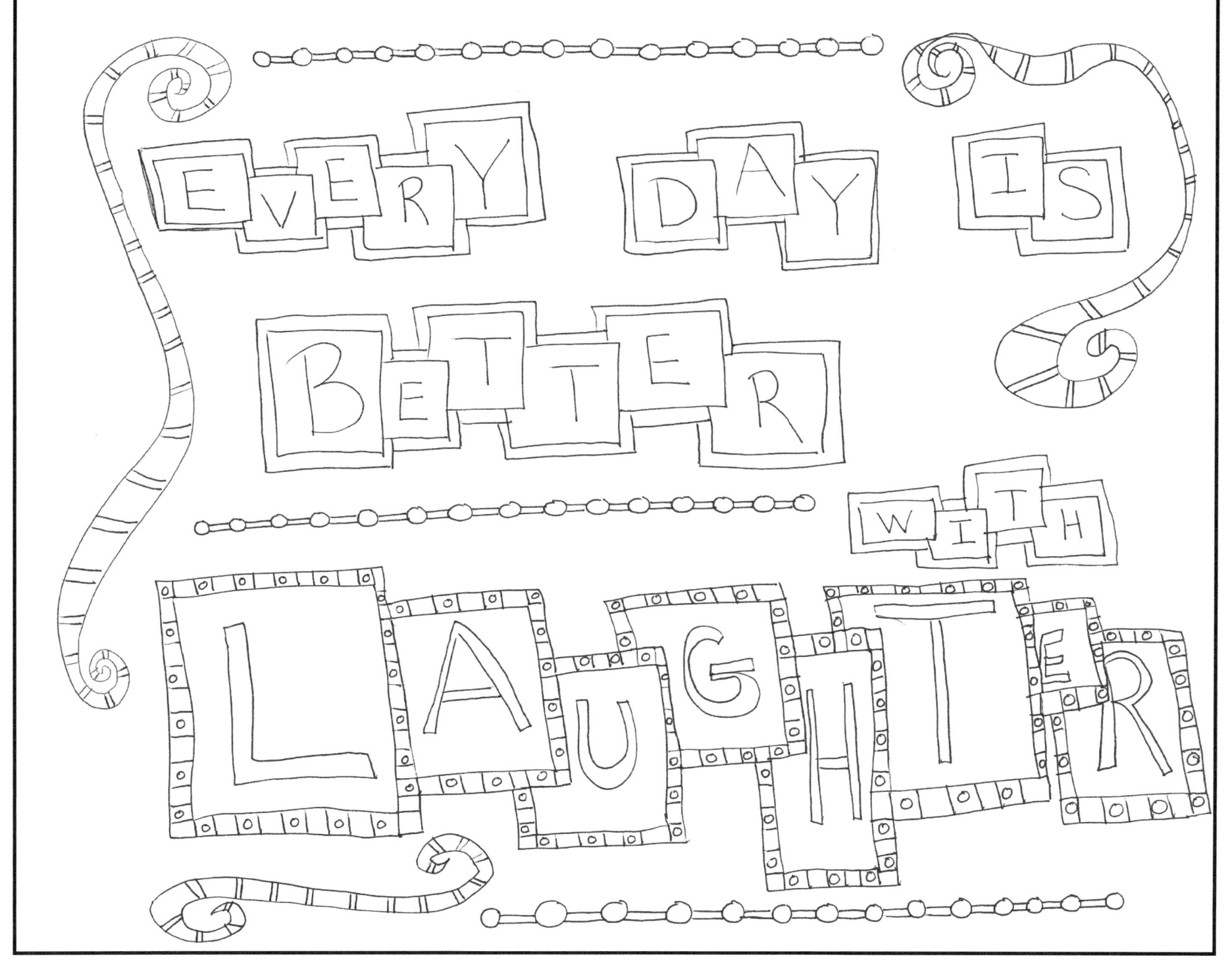

LAUGH while you color ... and have FUN!

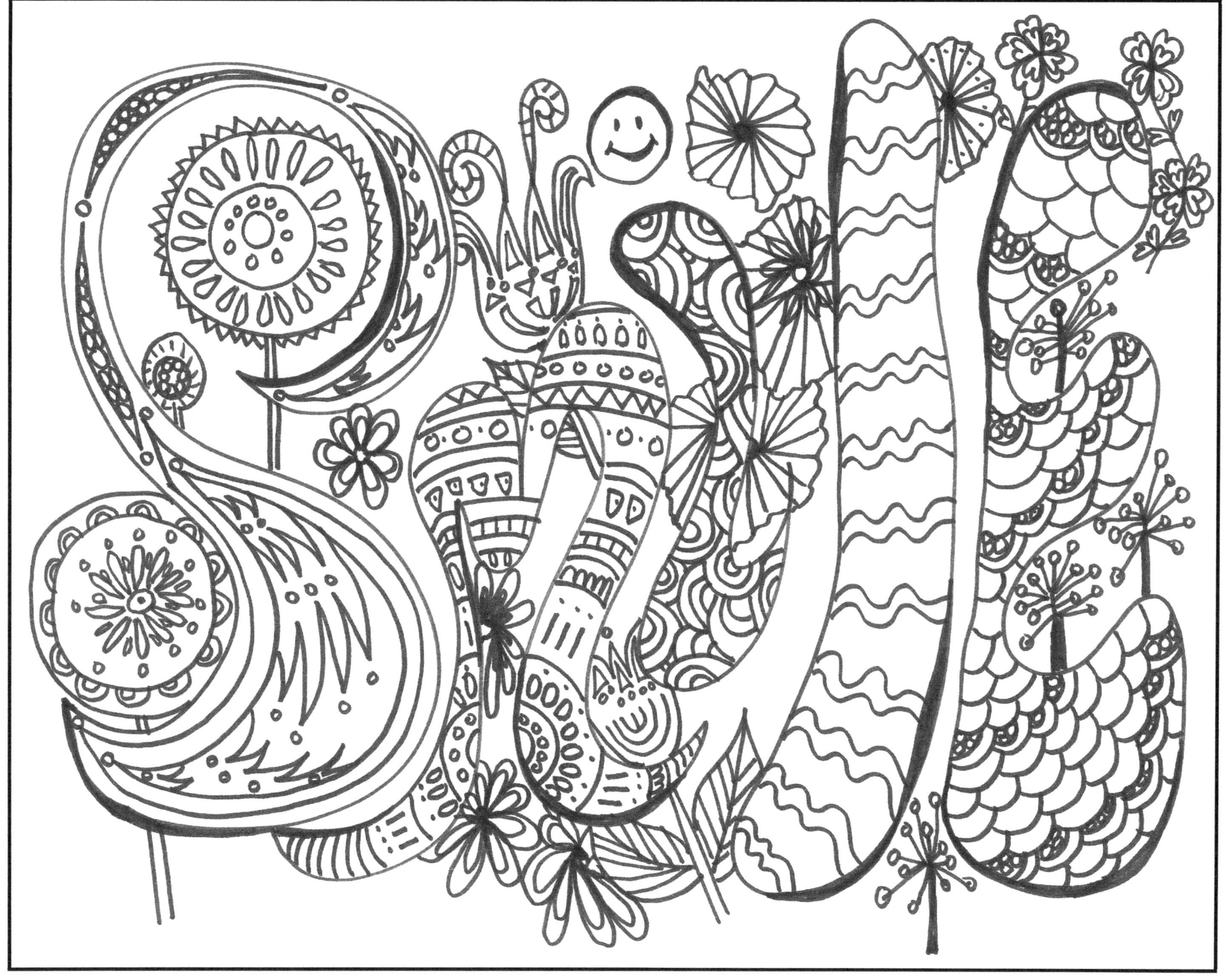

LAUGH while you color ... and smile with each color

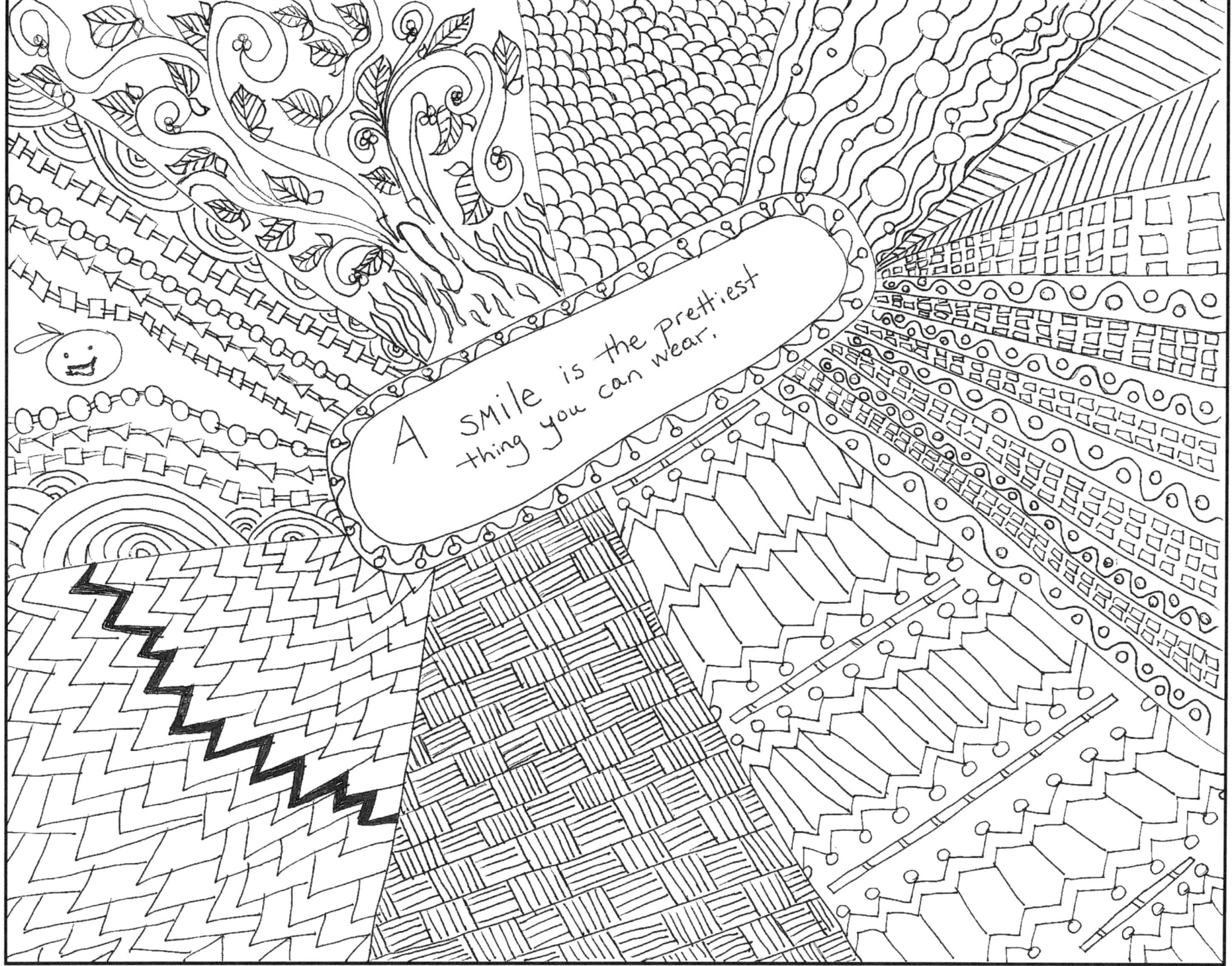

LAUGH while you color ... and share it with a friend

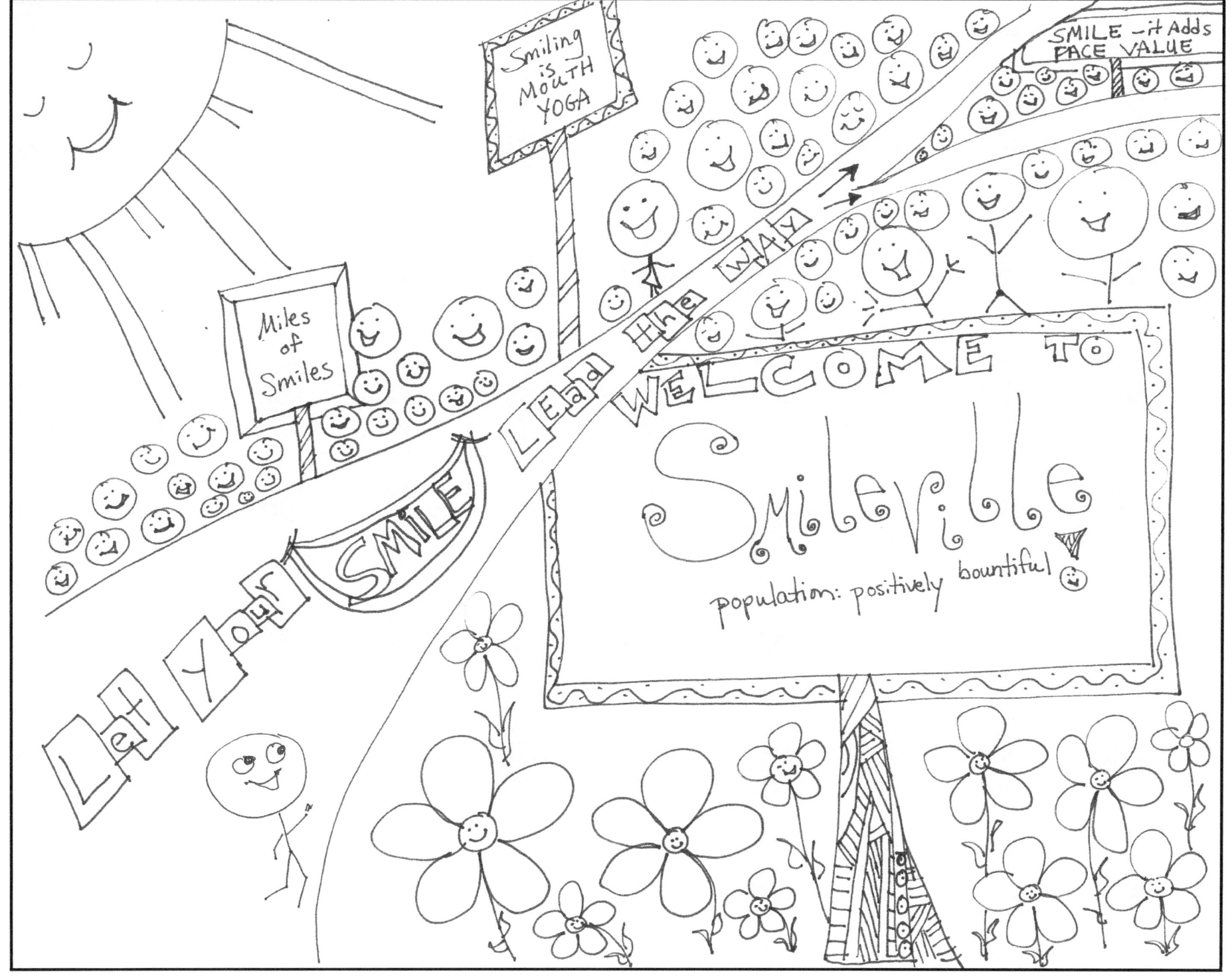

LAUGH while you color ... and let your imagination flourish

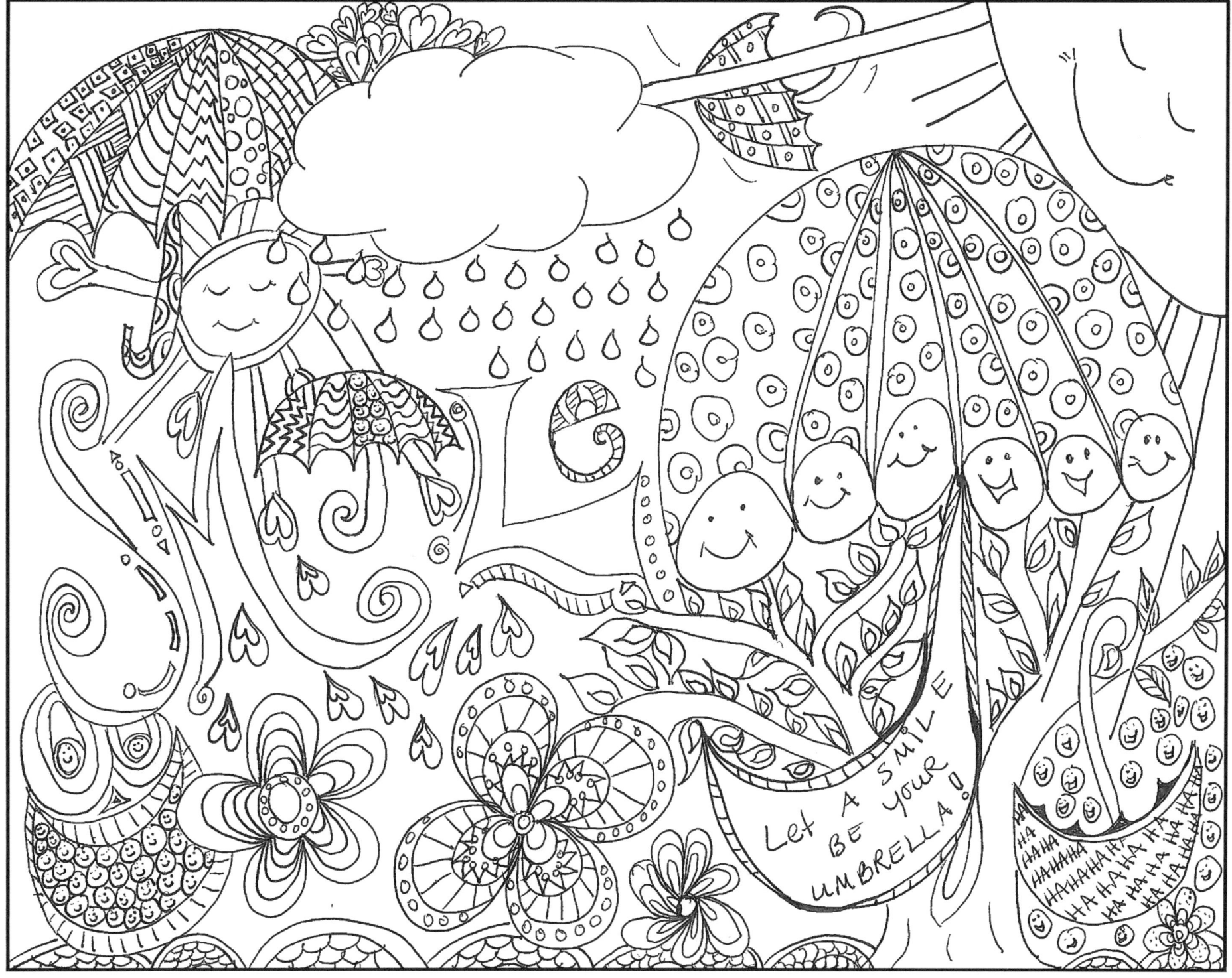

LAUGH while you color ... and relax and unwind

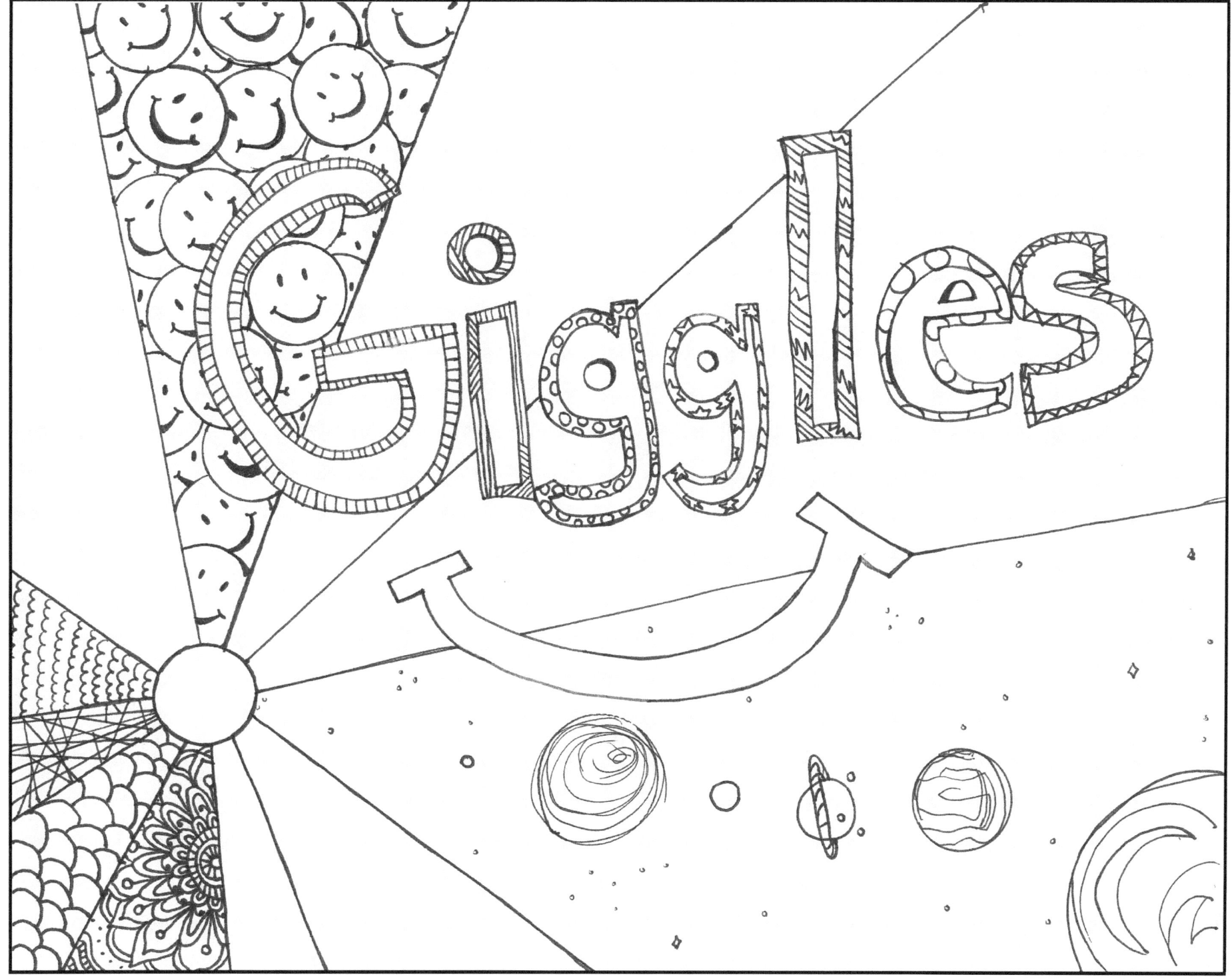

LAUGH while you color ... and increase your focus

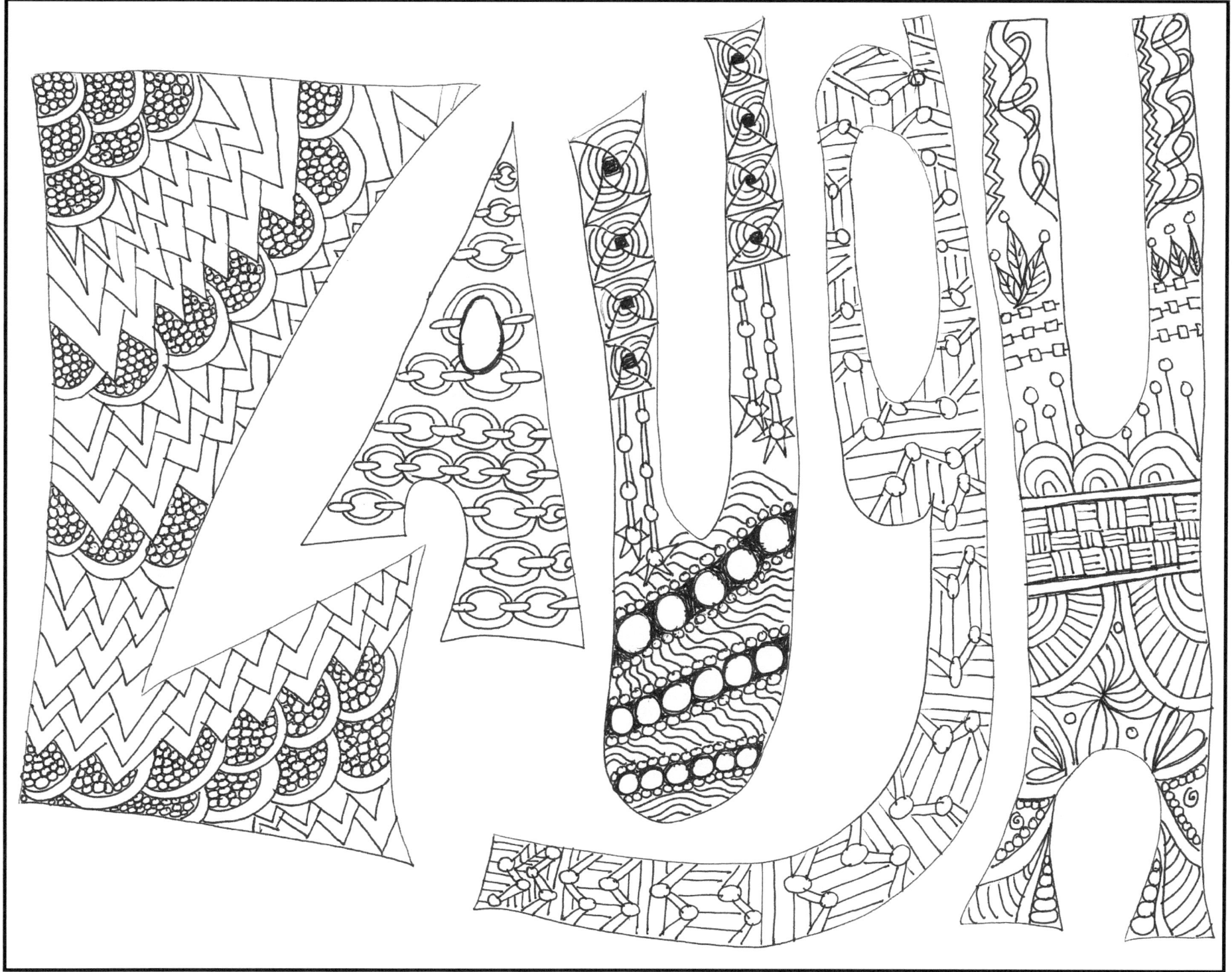

LAUGH while you color ... and improve your health

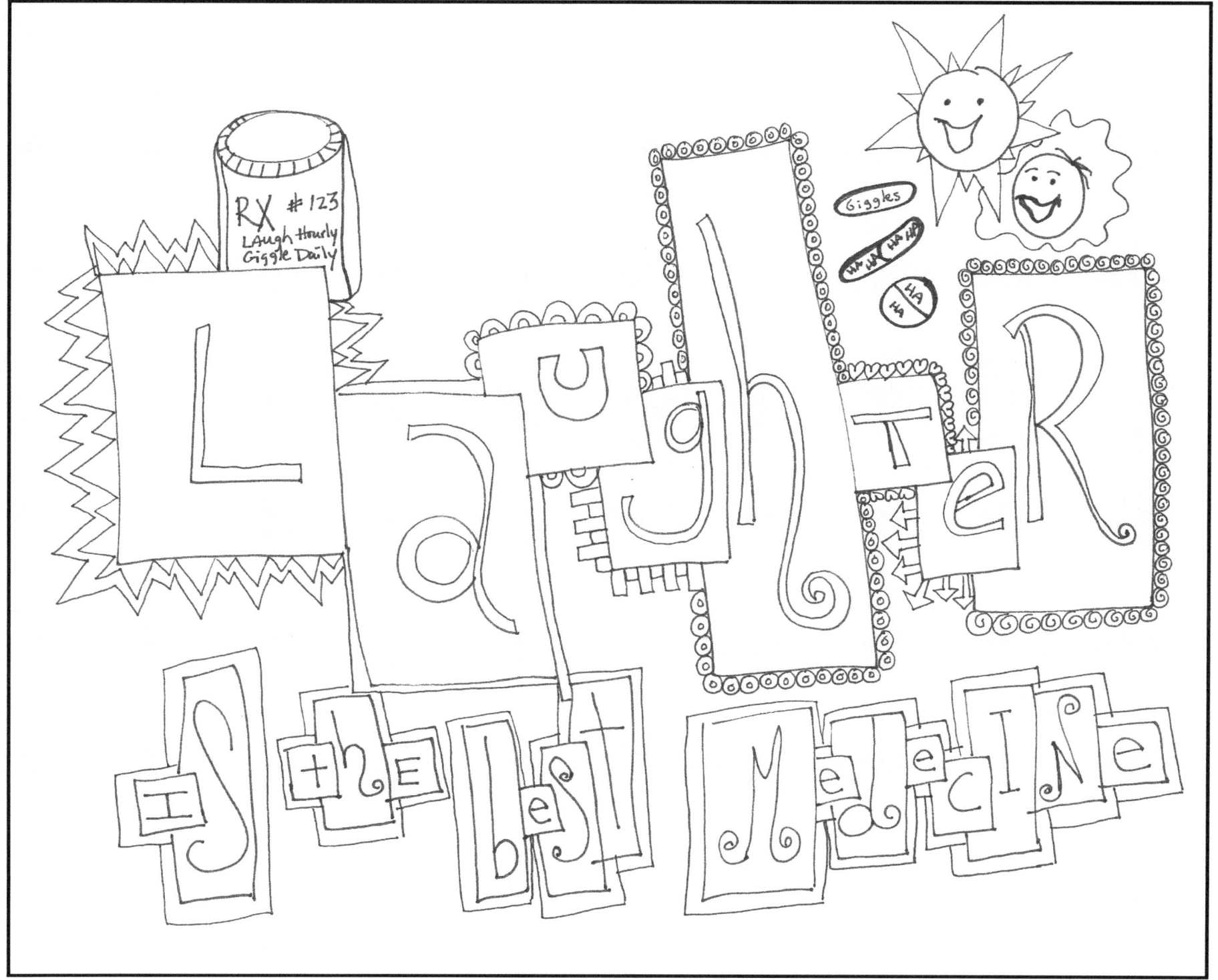

LAUGH while you color ... and get entered

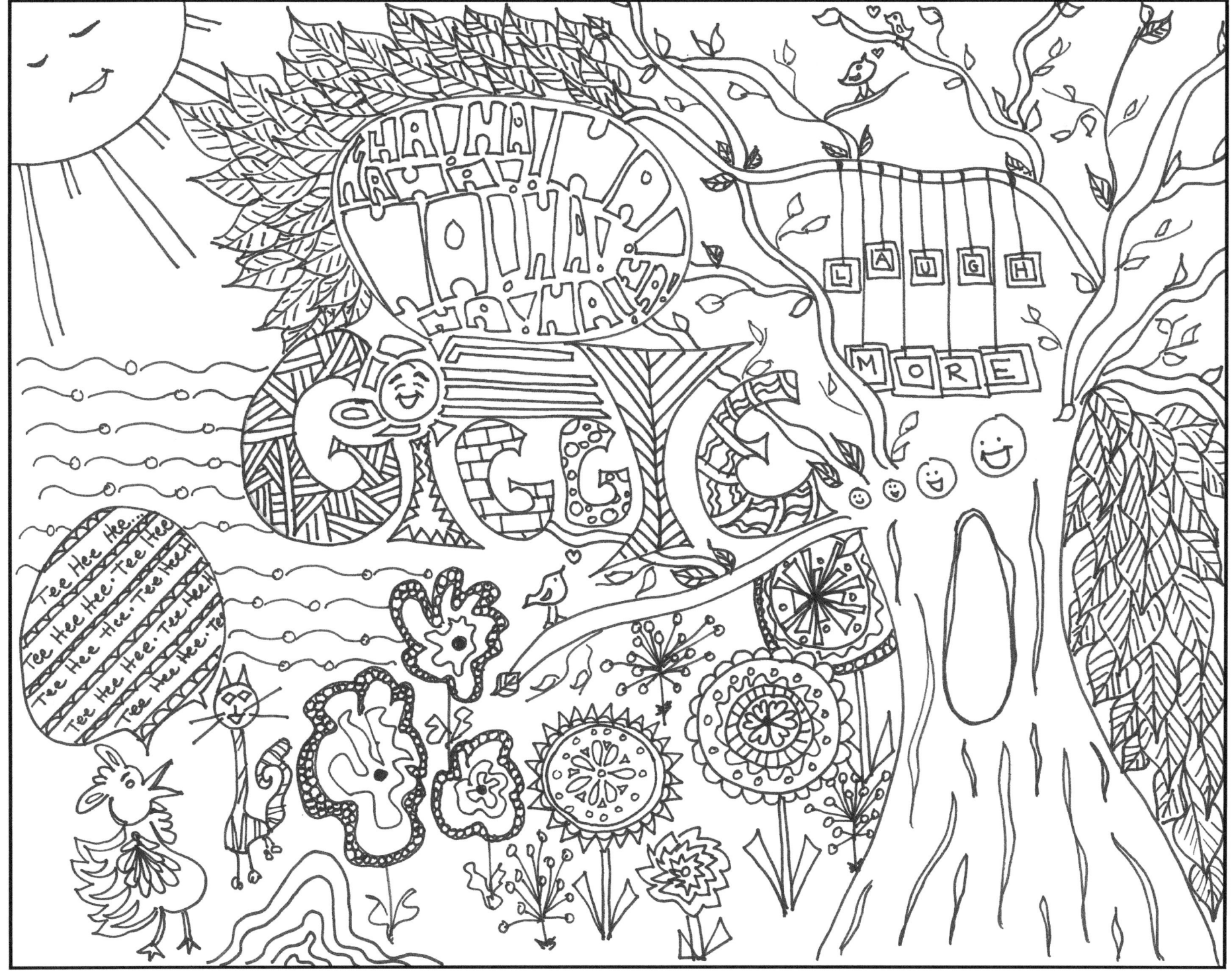

LAUGH while you color ... and explore your feelings

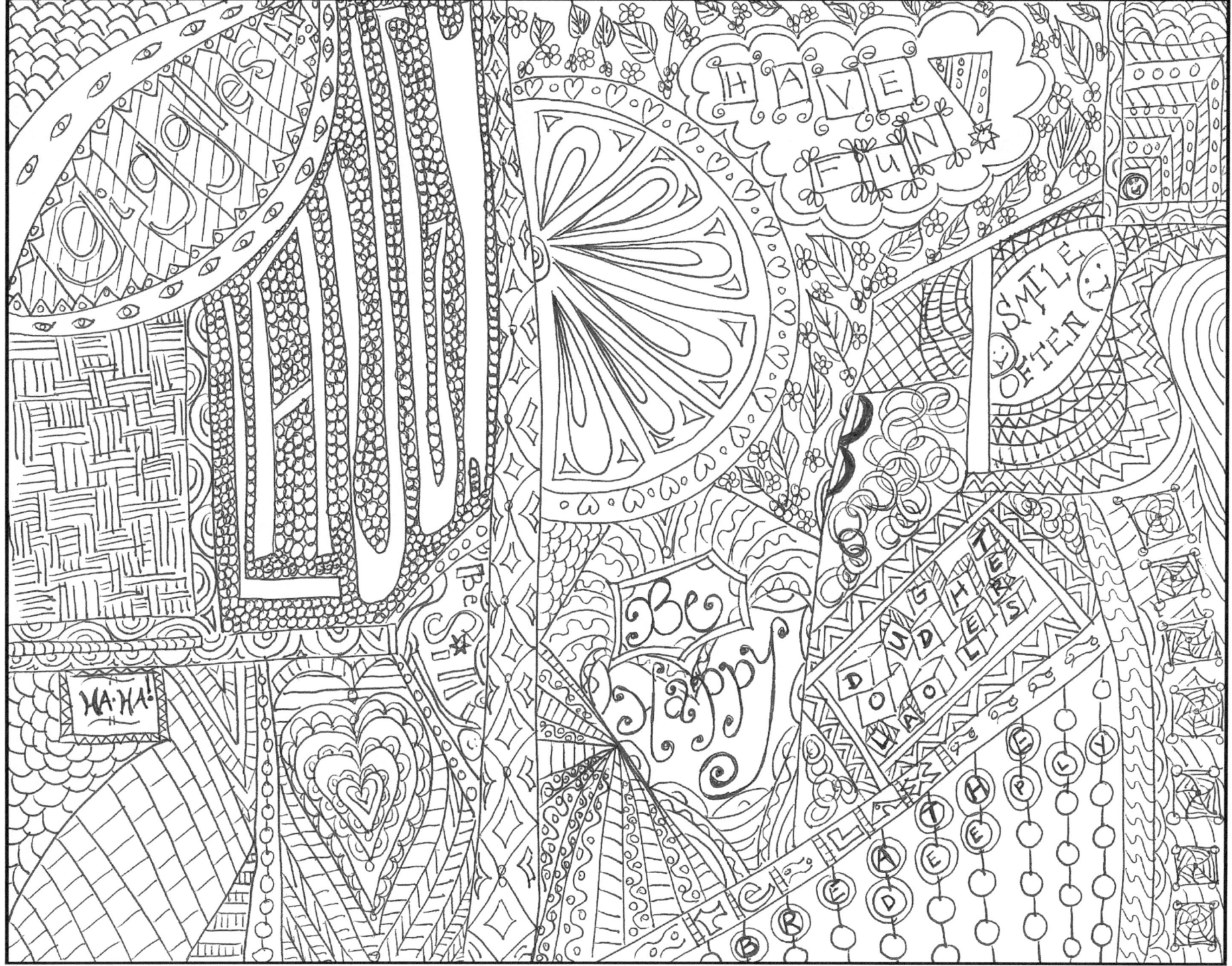

LAUGH while you color ... and savor the moment

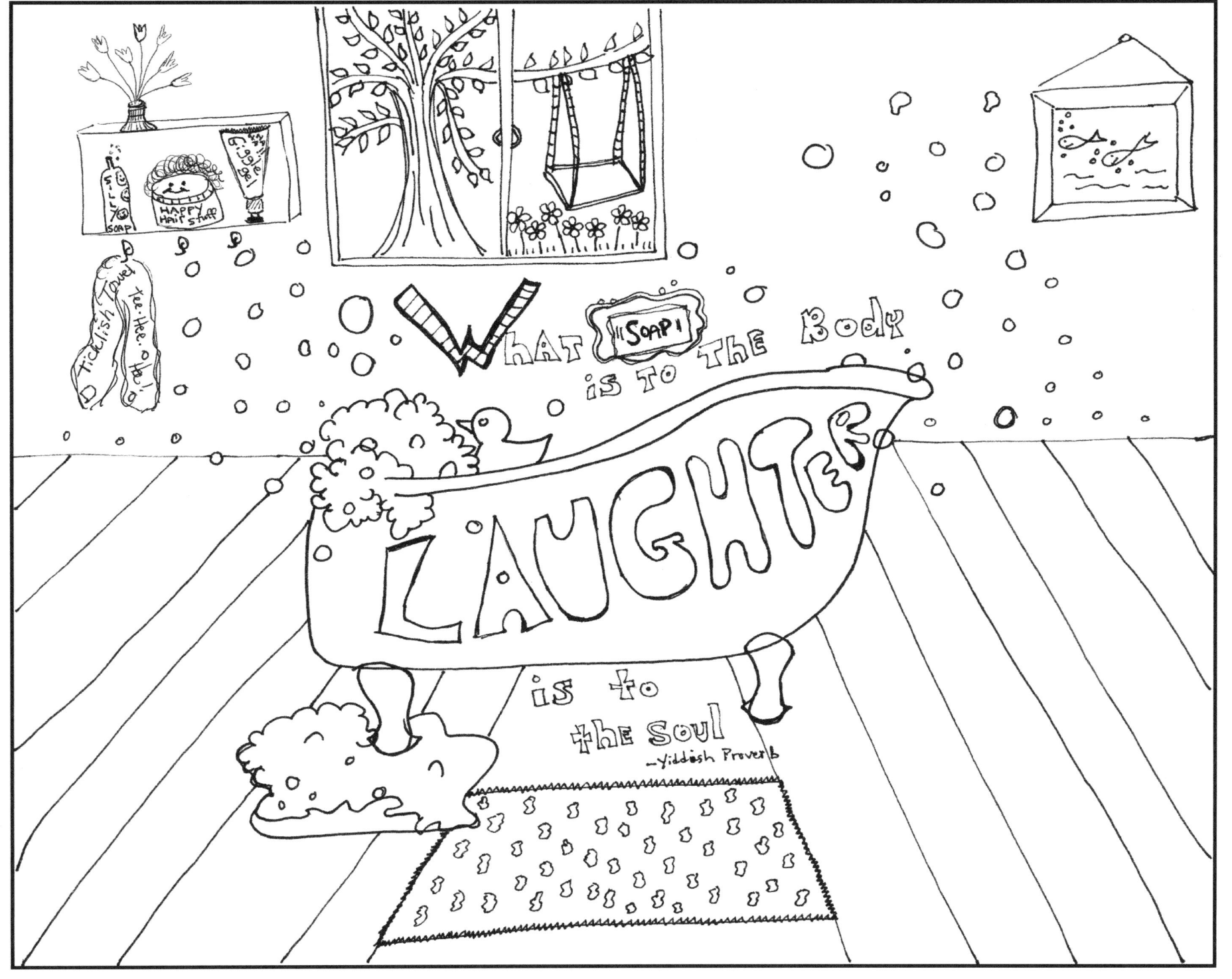

LAUGH while you color ... and notice how happy you feel

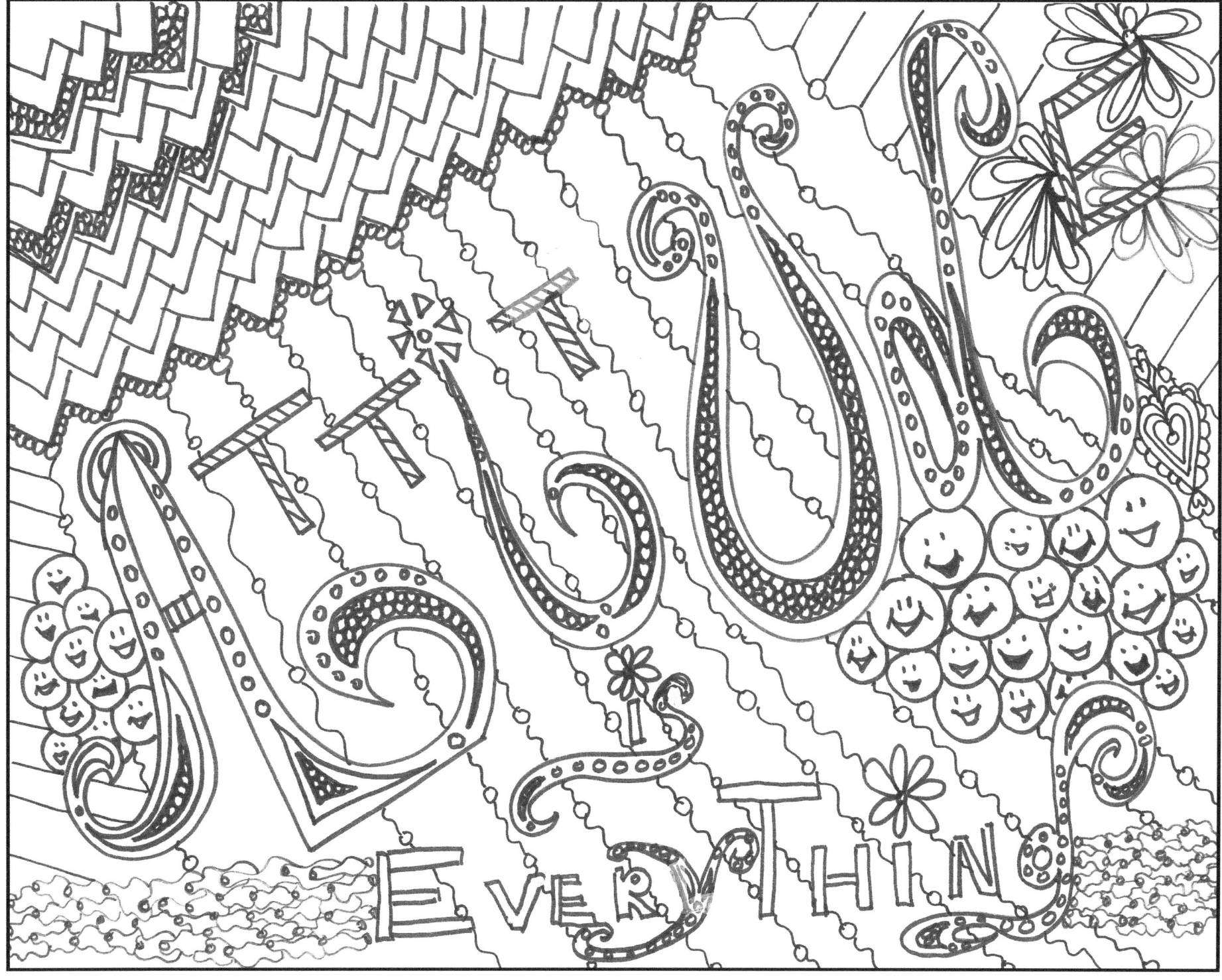

LAUGH while you color ... and discover yourself

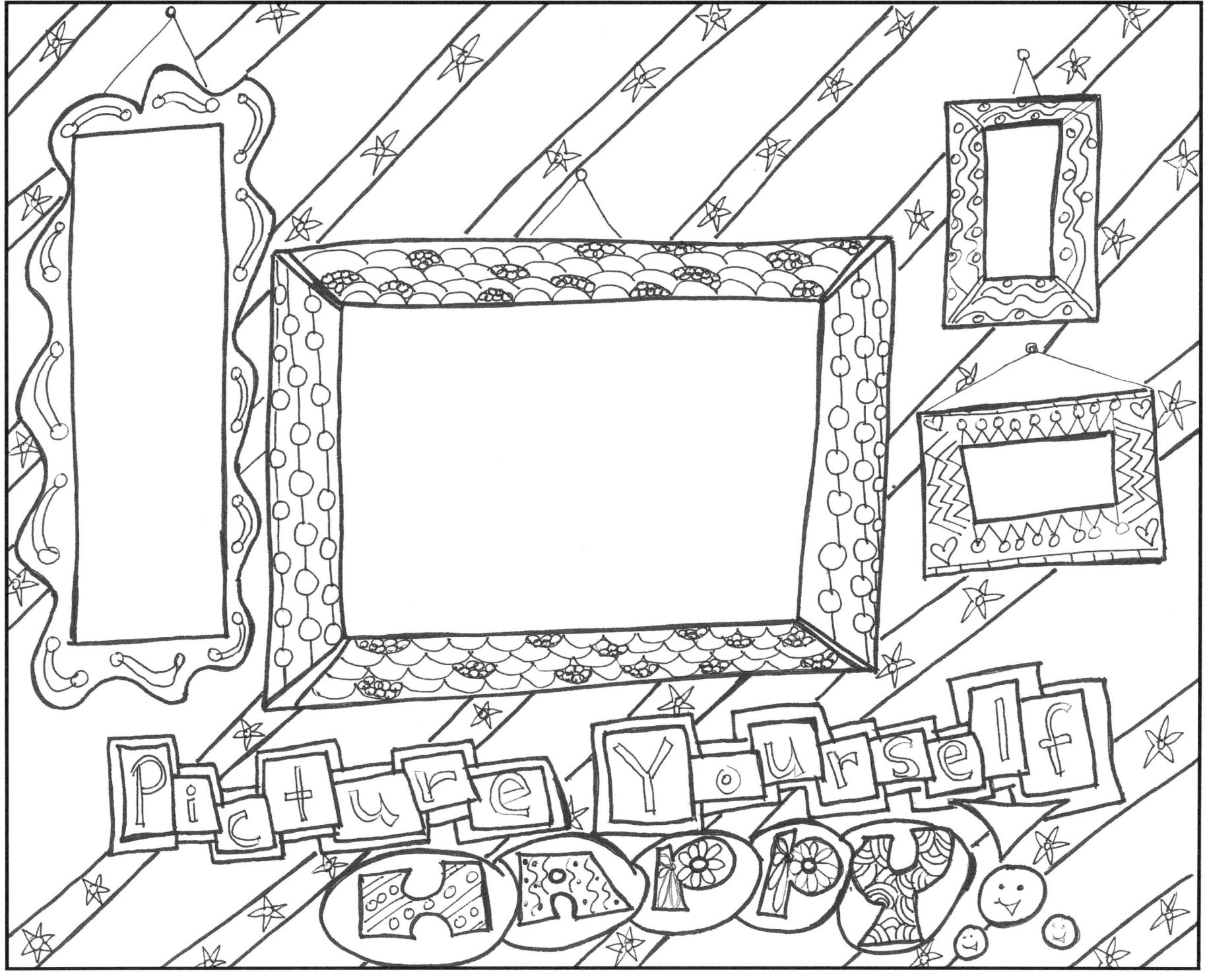

LAUGH while you color ... and relax for a great day

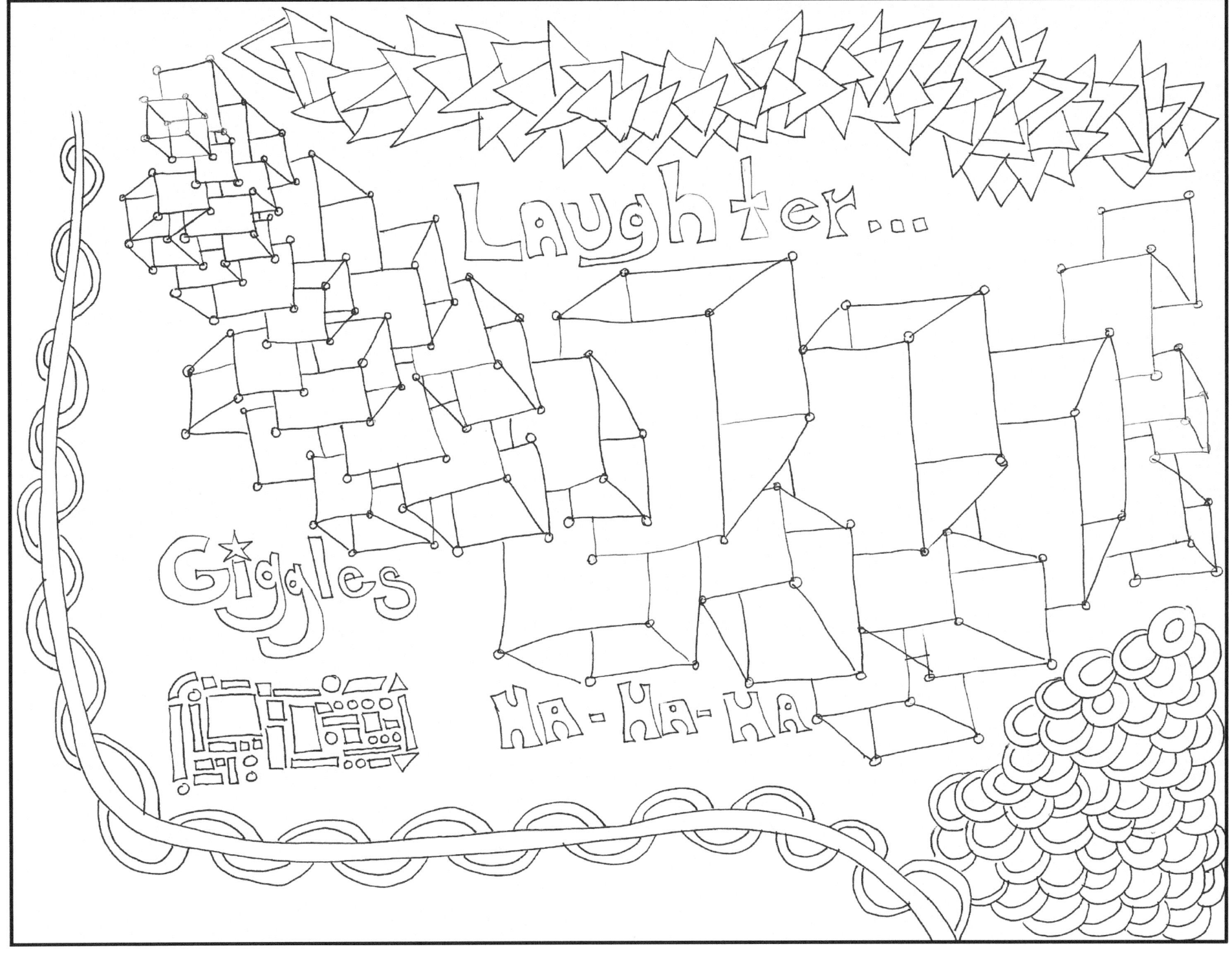

LAUGH while you color ... and feel your whole body relax

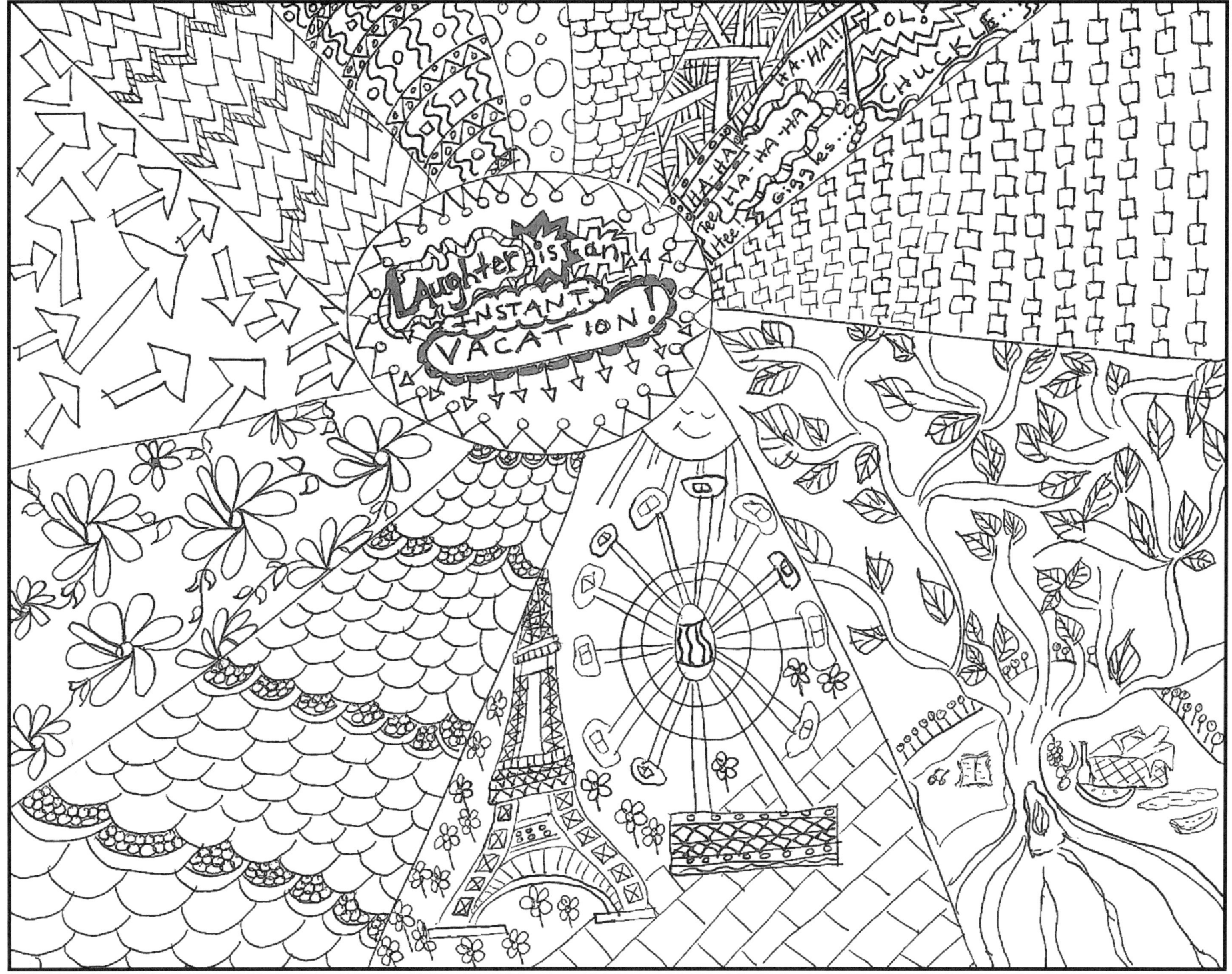

LAUGH while you color ... and let out your inner child

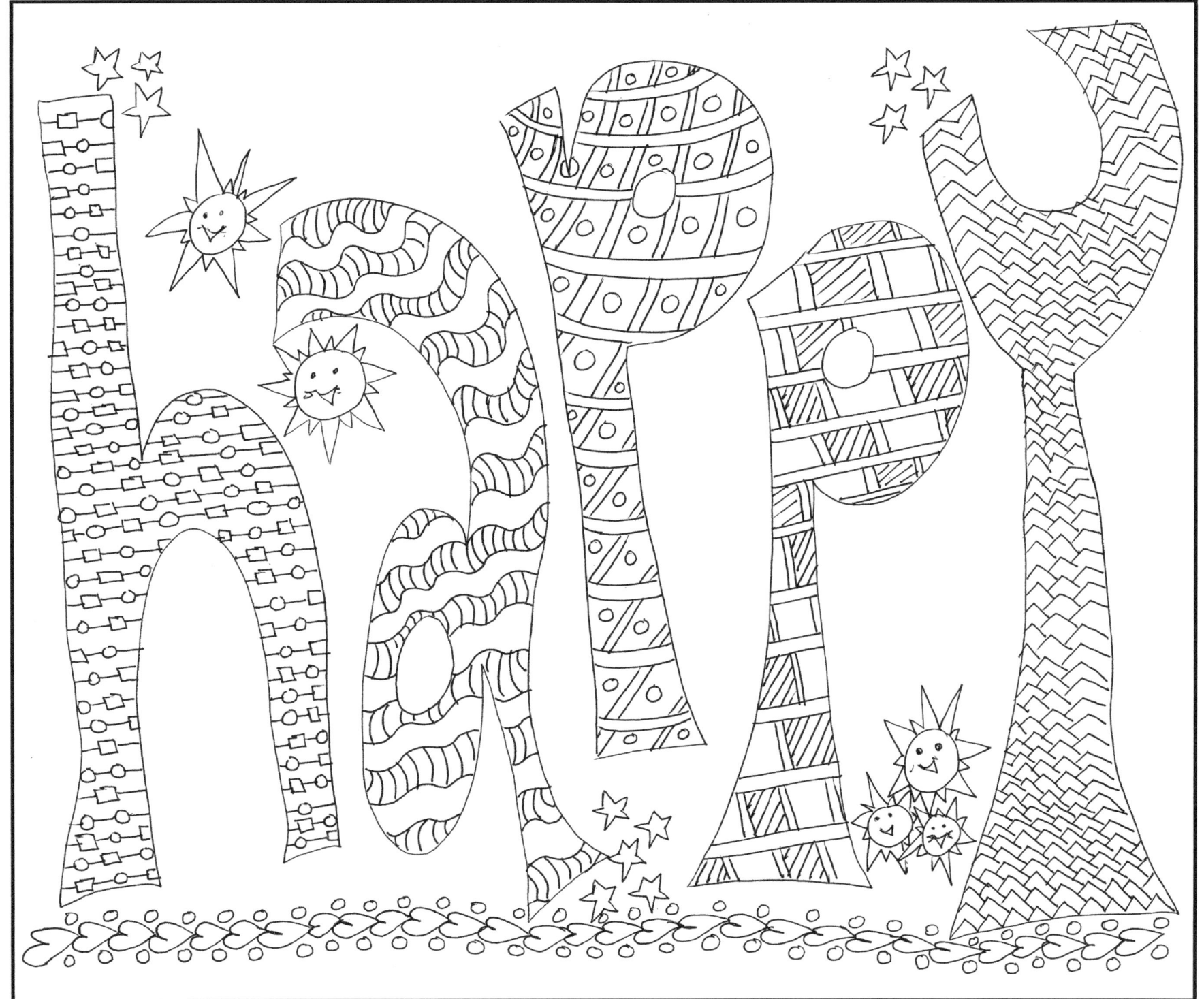

LAUGH while you color ... and express yourself

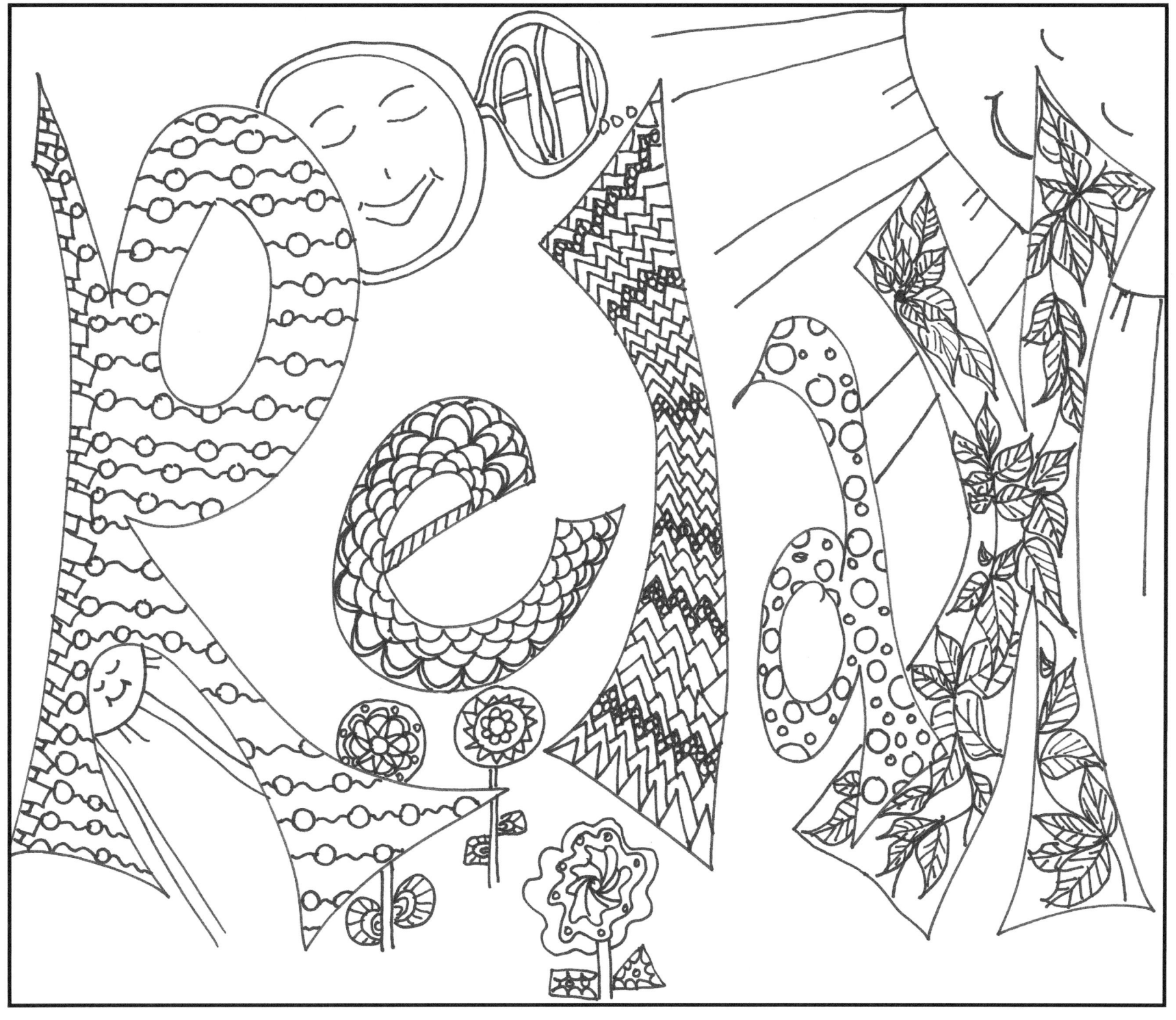

LAUGH while you color ... and unwind after a long day

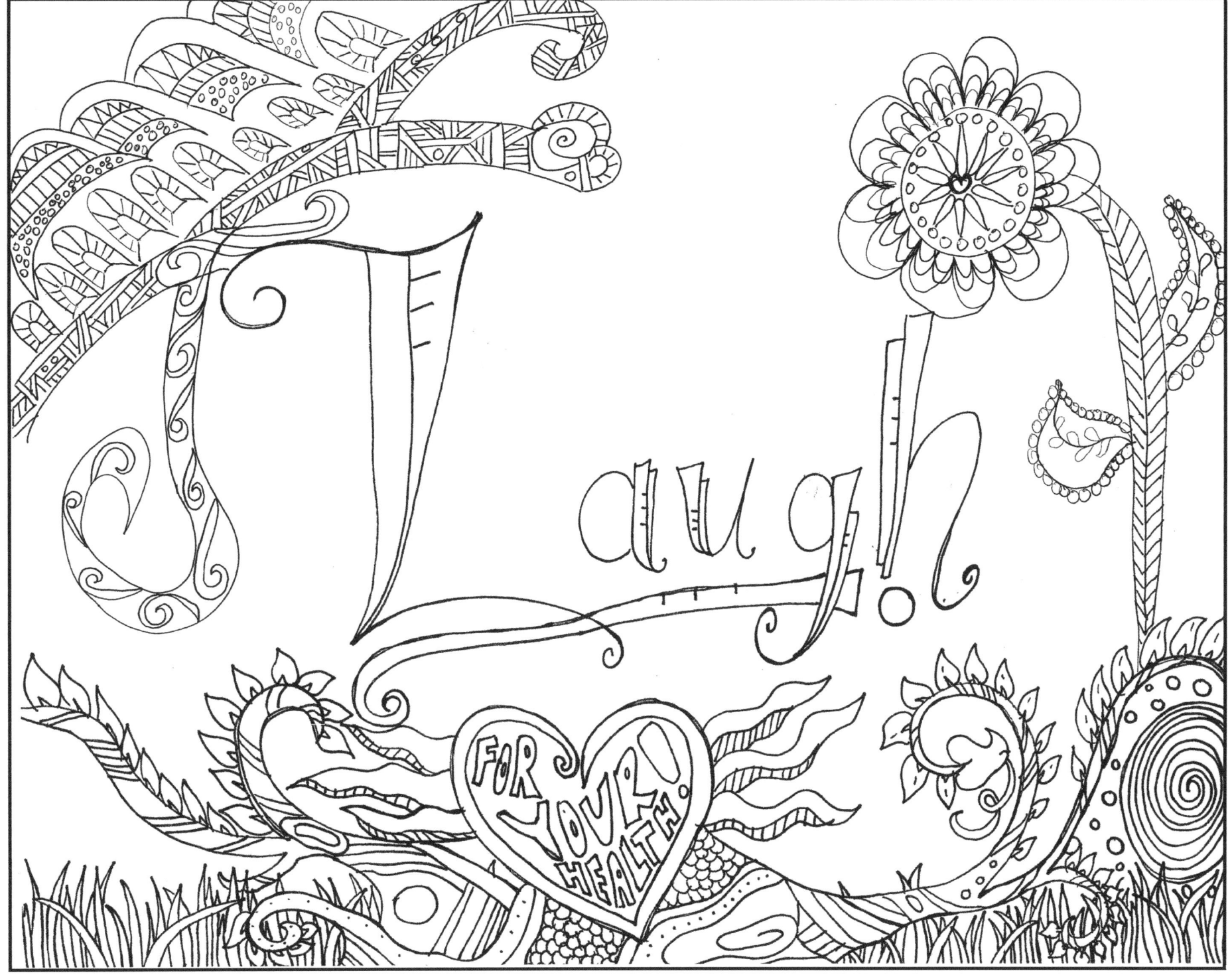

LAUGH while you color ... and feel happier and healthier

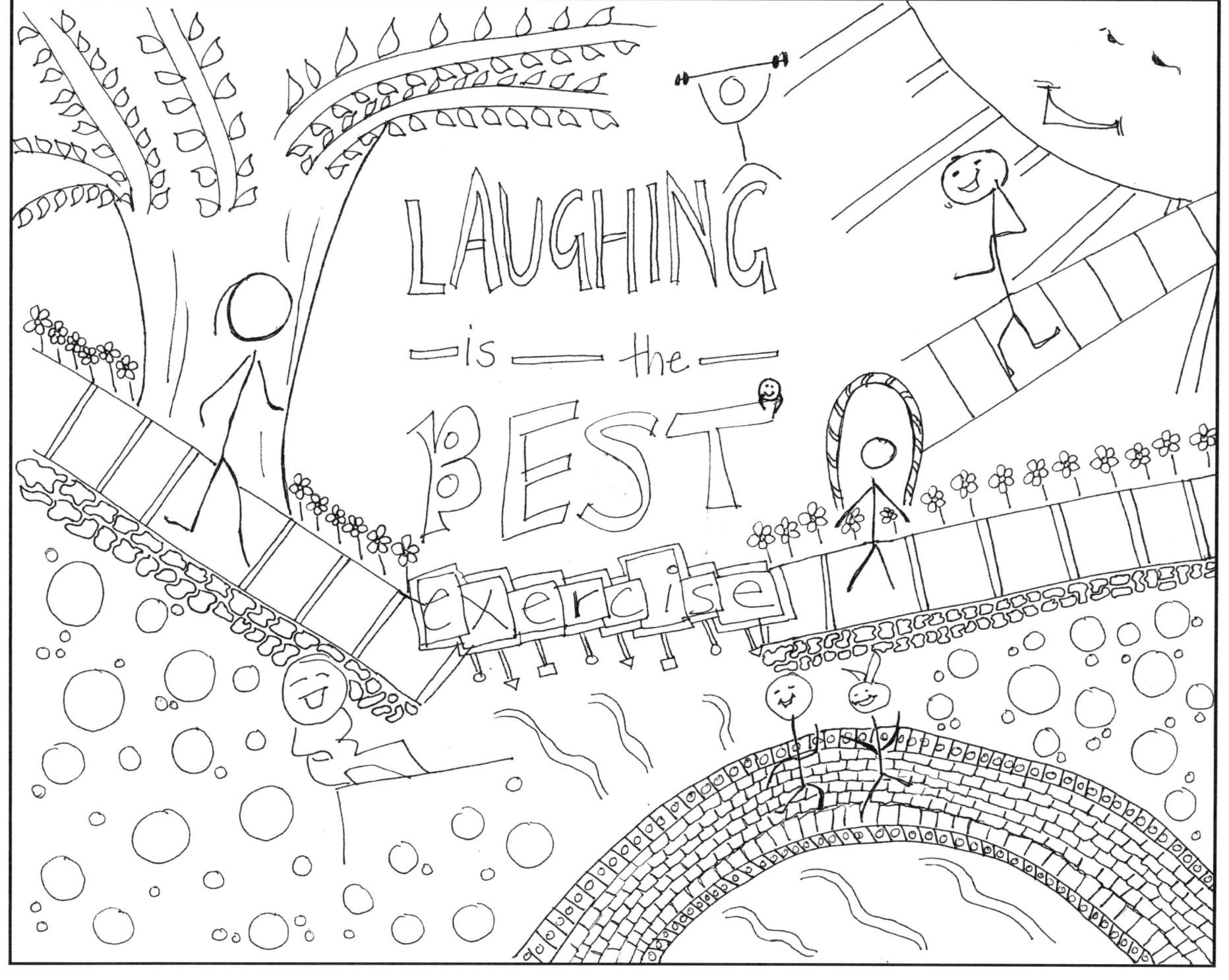

LAUGH while you color ... and tap into your childlike silliness

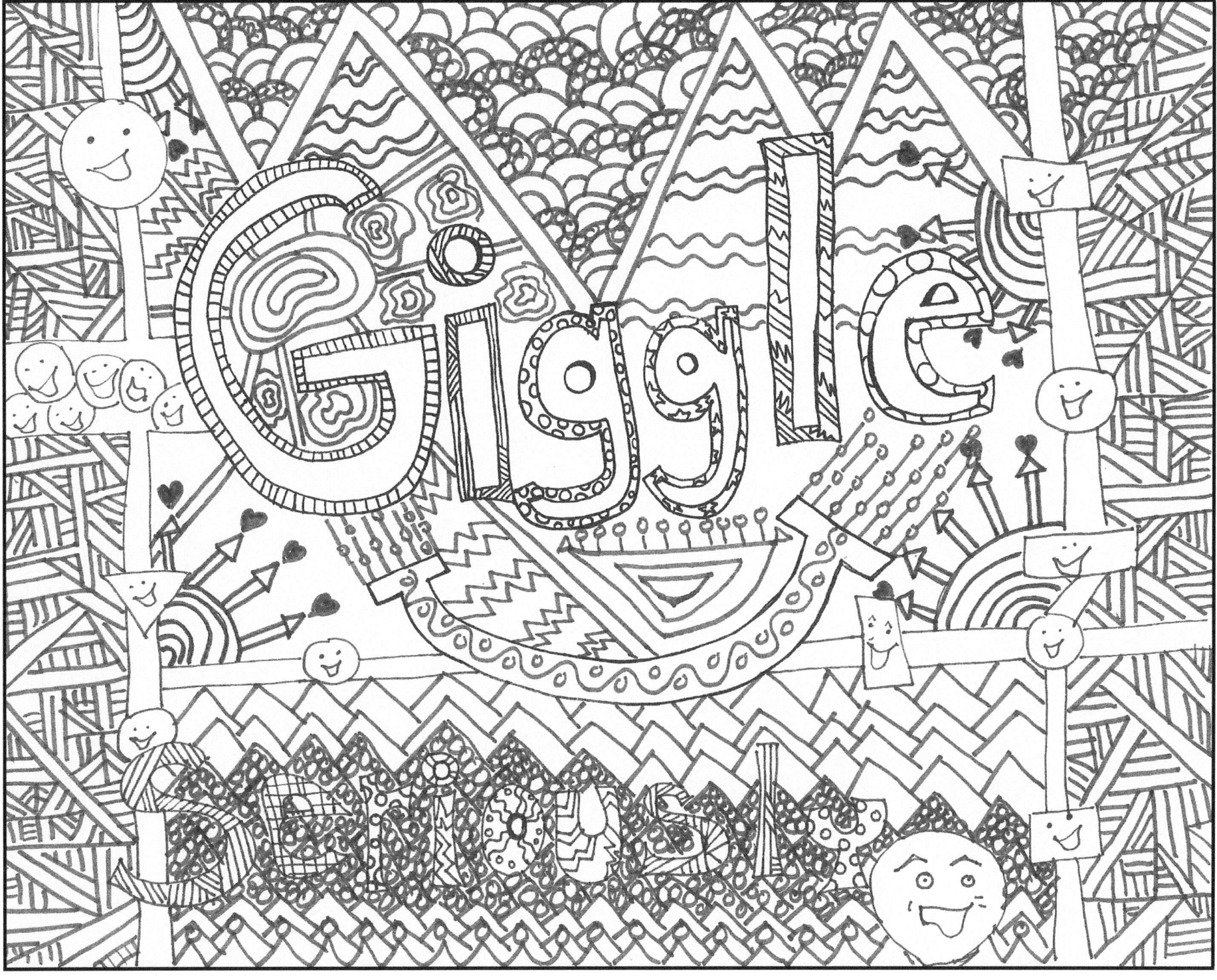

LAUGH while you color ... and invite a friend to join you

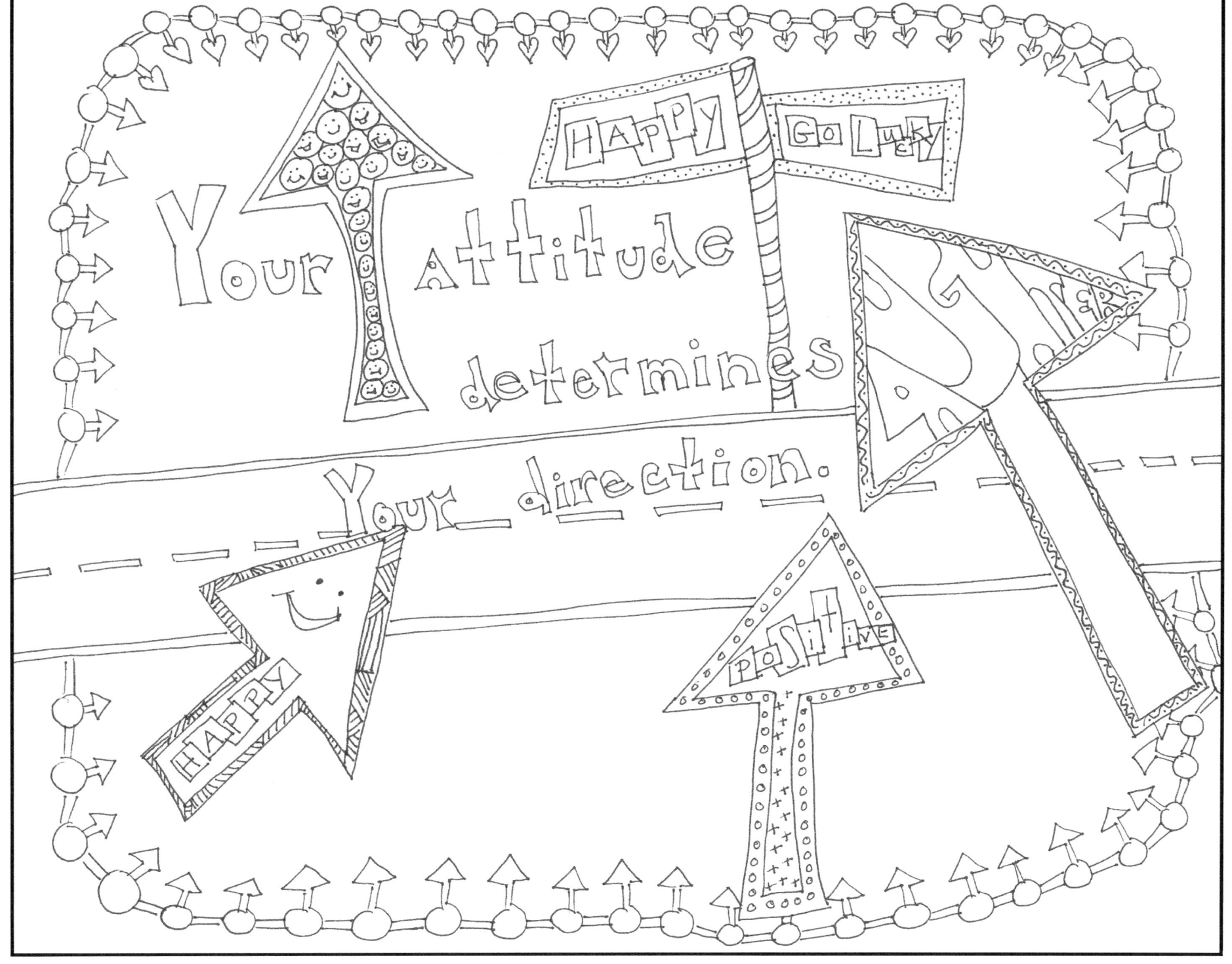

LAUGH while you color ... and encourage your creativity

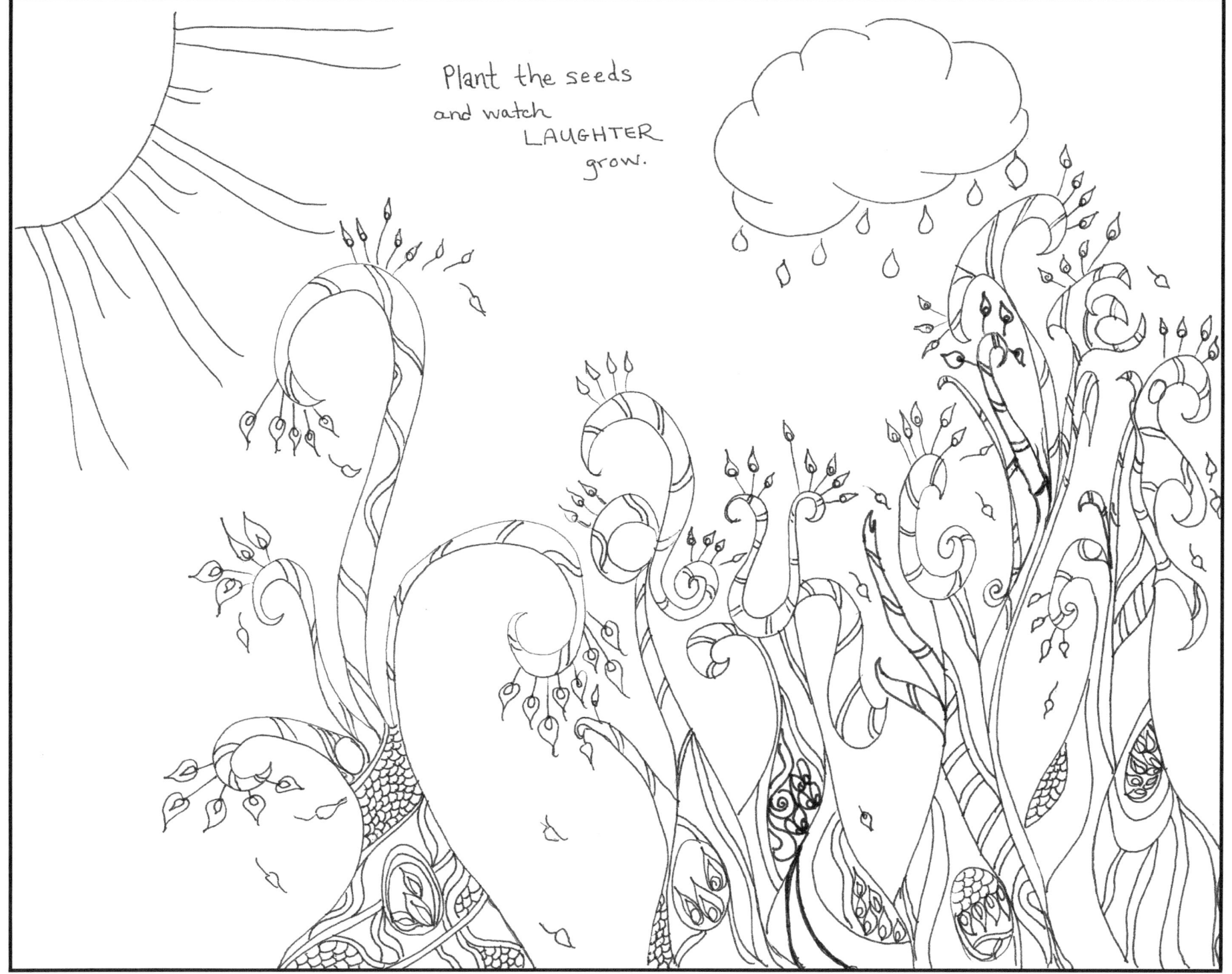

LAUGH while you color ... and celebrate your accomplishments

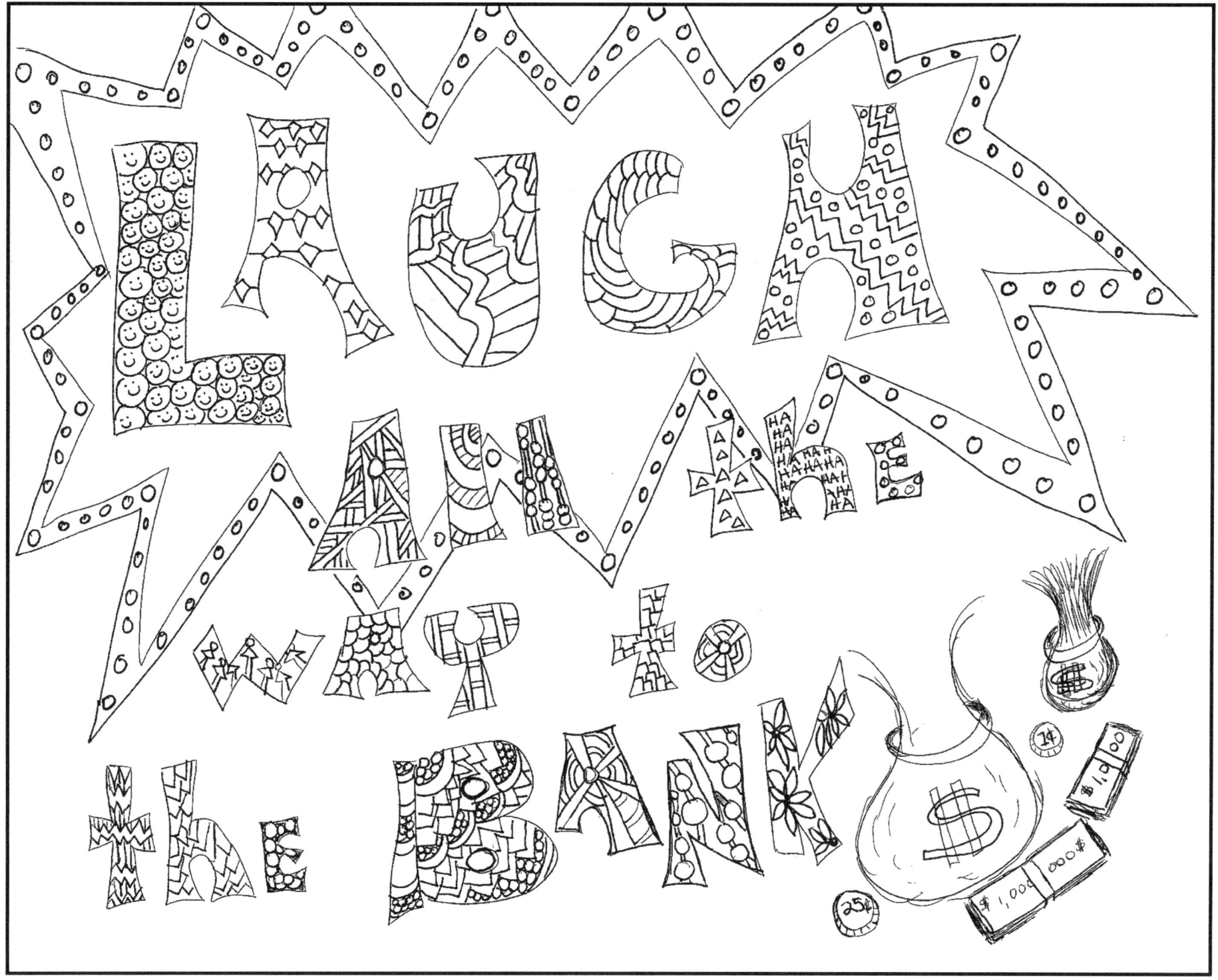

LAUGH while you color ... and explore your feelings

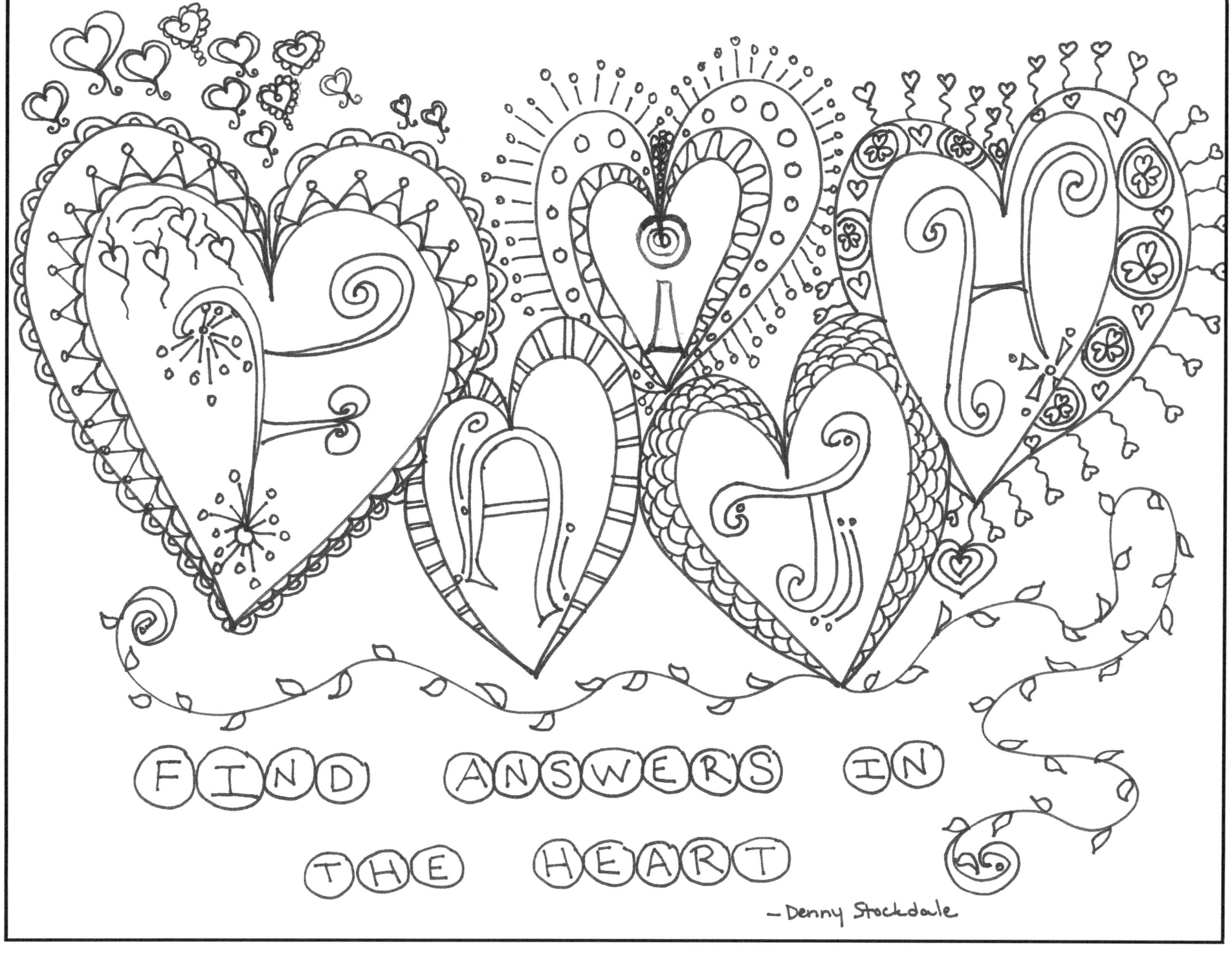

FIND ANSWERS IN THE HEART

—Denny Stockdale

LAUGH while you color ... and feel good all over

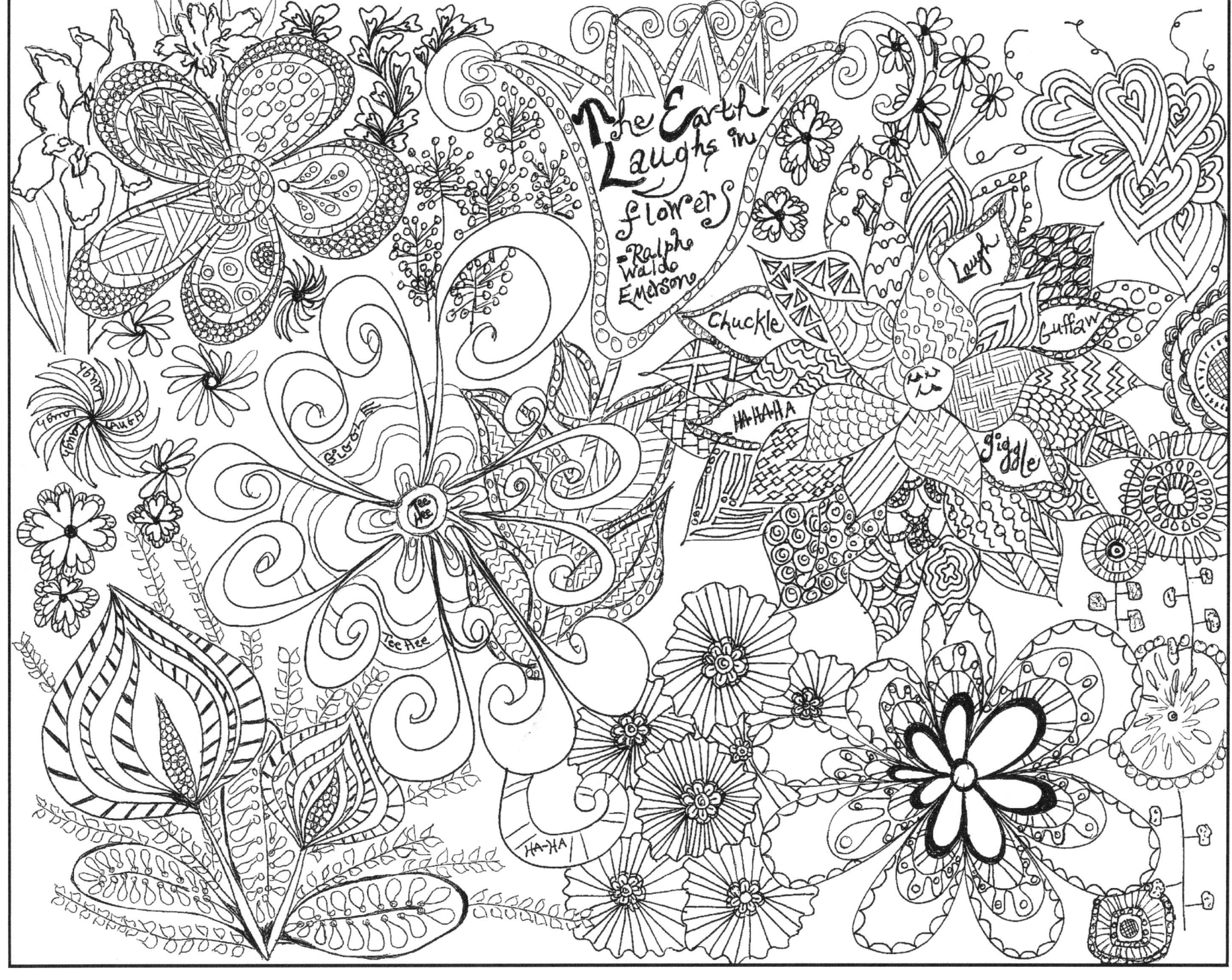

LAUGH while you color ... and become more mindful

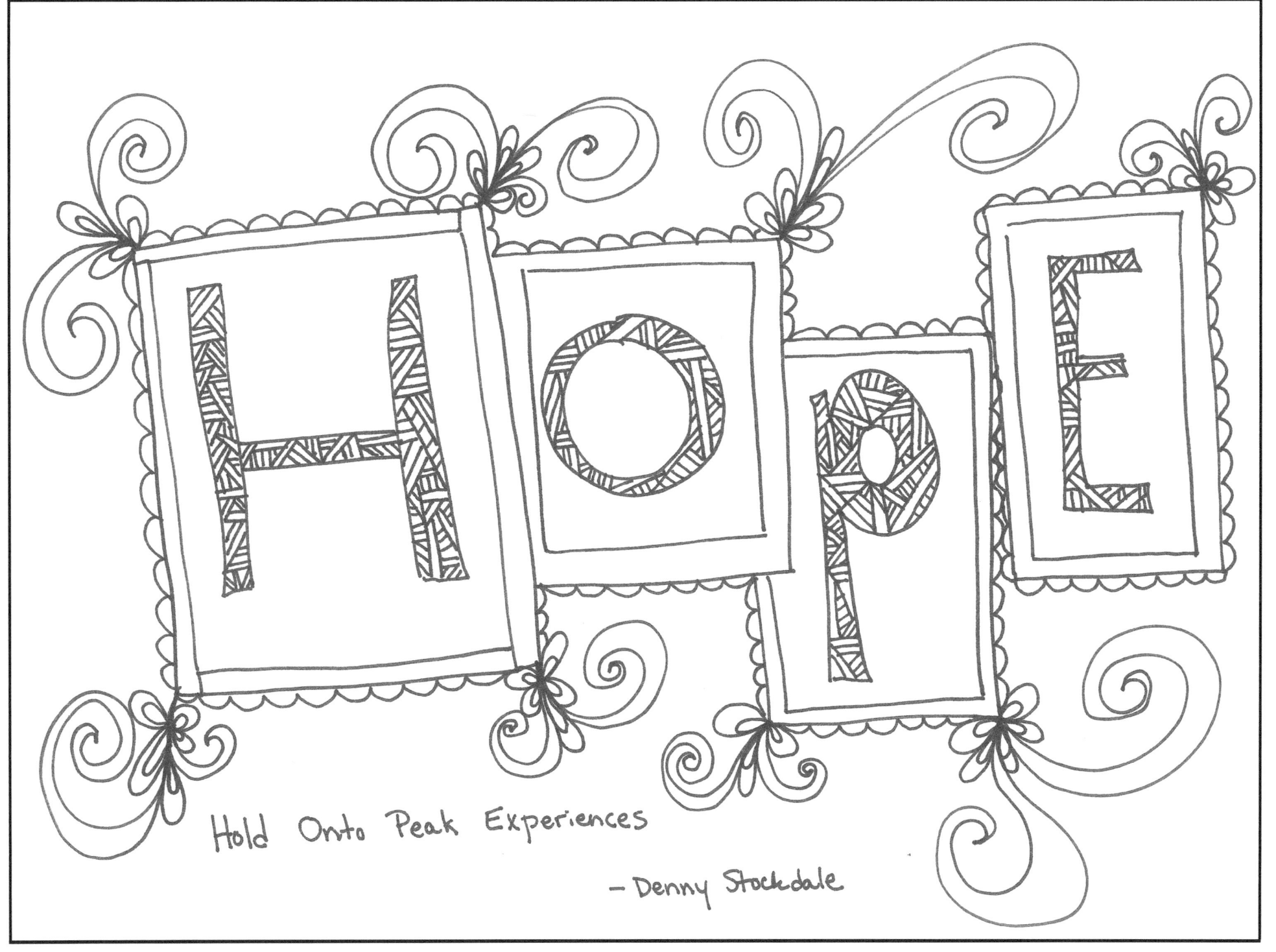

Hold Onto Peak Experiences

— Denny Stockdale

LAUGH while you color ... and giggle with glee

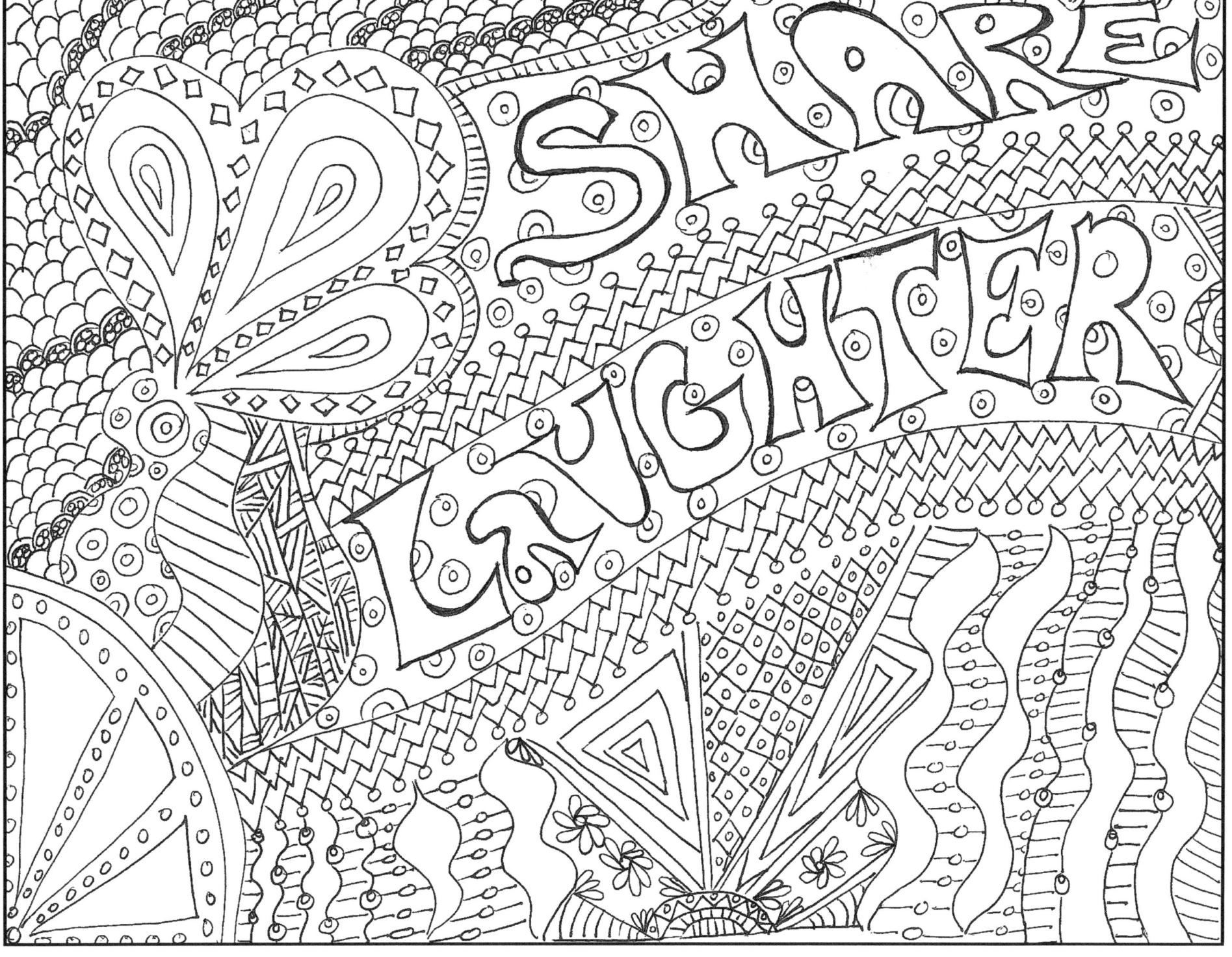

LAUGH while you color ... and spread the joy

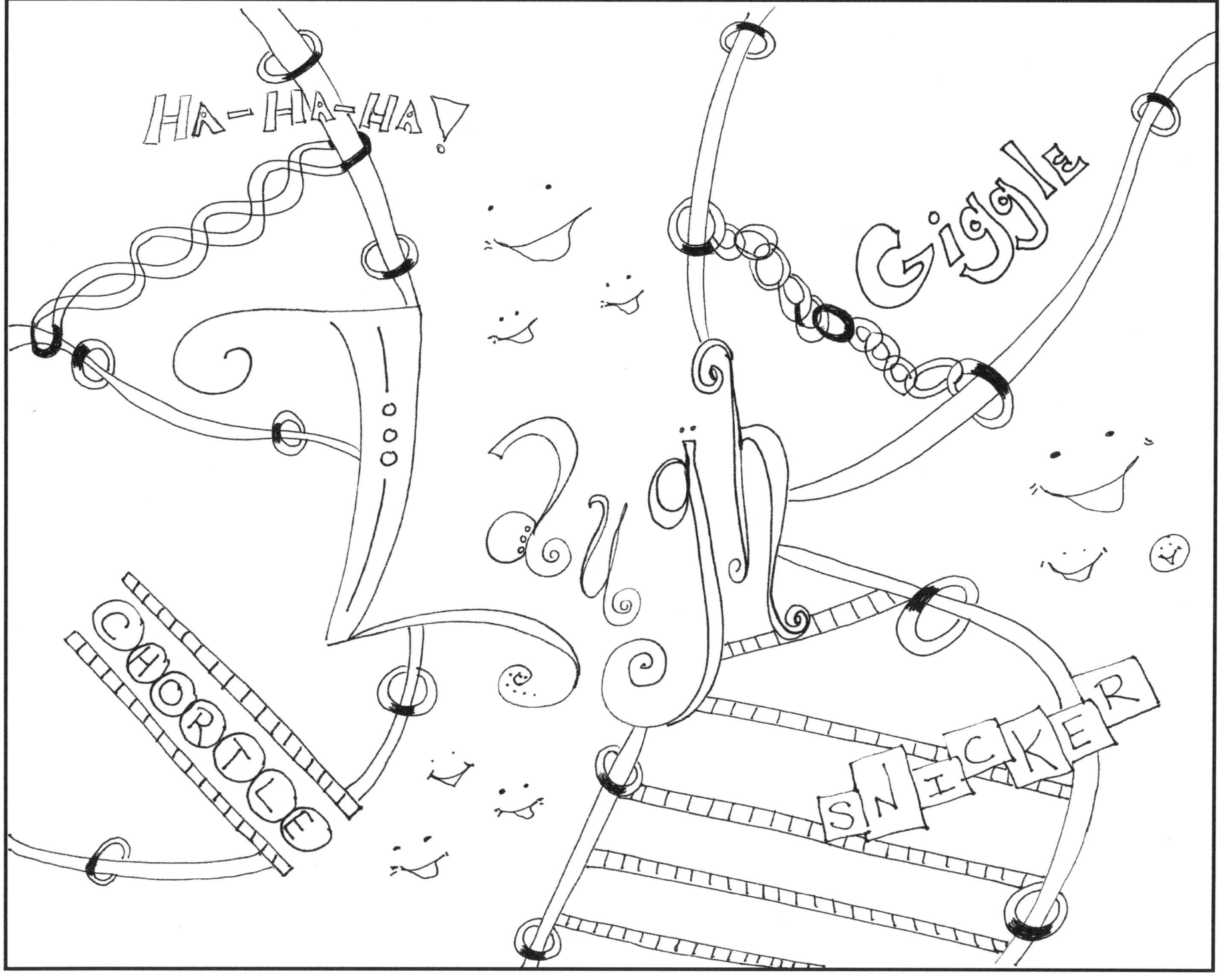

LAUGH while you color ... and find a happy calm

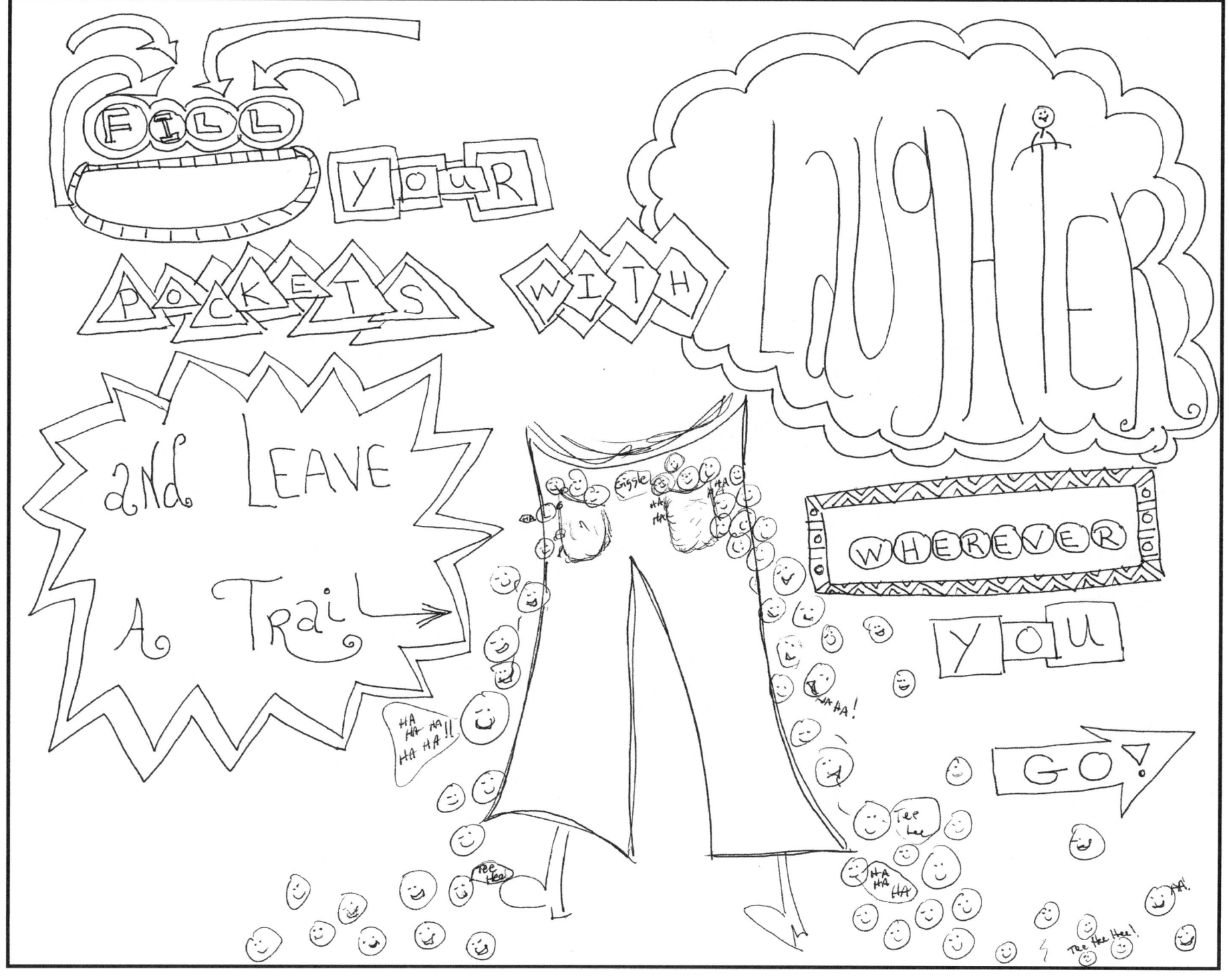

Create your own "Laughter Doodle", right here for a chance to
win a featured page in my next Laughter Doodles coloring book.

Visit the submissions page at: www.LaughterDoodles.com

Create your own "Laughter Doodle" right here for a chance to win a featured page in my next Laughter Doodles coloring book.

Visit the submissions page at: www.LaughterDoodles.com

Create your own "Laughter Doodle" right here for a chance to win a featured page in my next Laughter Doodles coloring book,

Visit the submissions page at: www,LaughterDoodles,com

Create your own "Laughter Doodle" right here for a chance to win a featured page in my next Laughter Doodles coloring book.

Visit the submissions page at: www.LaughterDoodles.com

Create your own "Laughter Doodle" right here for a chance to win a featured page in my next Laughter Doodles coloring book.

Visit the submissions page at: www.LaughterDoodles.com

Create your own "Laughter Doodle" right here for a chance to win a featured page in my next Laughter Doodles coloring book.

Visit the submissions page at: www.LaughterDoodles.com

Create your own "Laughter Doodle" right here for a chance to win a featured page in my next Laughter Doodles coloring book.

Visit the submissions page at: www.LaughterDoodles.com

Create your own "Laughter Doodle" right here for a chance to win a featured page in my next Laughter Doodles coloring book.

Visit the submissions page at: www.LaughterDoodles.com

Create your own "Laughter Doodle" right here for a chance to win a featured page in my next Laughter Doodles coloring book.

Visit the submissions page at: www.LaughterDoodles.com

Create your own "Laughter Doodle" right here for a chance to win a featured page in my next Laughter Doodles coloring book.

Visit the submissions page at: www.LaughterDoodles.com